Editorial Project Manager
Eric Migliaccio

Editor in Chief
Karen J. Goldfluss, M.S. Ed.

Creative Director
Sarah M. Fournier

Cover Artist
Barb Lorseyedi

Illustrator
Clint McKnight

Art Coordinator
Renée Mc Elwee

Imaging
Amanda R. Harter

Publisher
Mary D. Smith, M.S. Ed.

S0-DFJ-949

GRADES 6-7

Using Paired Novels to Build Close Reading Skills

Novels Featured in This Resource

A Long Walk to Water

Home of the Brave

- Meets close reading requirements through in-depth analysis, comparison, and synthesis of high-interest, award-winning contemporary novels
- Uses individual, collaborative, and linked learning activities to examine how authors approach key literary elements
- Encourages personal reader response through student-created Interactive Literature Notebooks
- Fosters deep discussion, use of textual evidence, and written responses to support ideas and opinions
- Correlated to the Common Core State Standards

Teacher Created Resources

Author
Janna Anderson, M.A.

CORRELATED TO COMMON CORE STANDARDS

For correlations to the Common Core State Standards, see pages 93–96 of this book or visit *http://www.teachercreated.com/standards/*.

Teacher Created Resources
6421 Industry Way
Westminster, CA 92683
www.teachercreated.com

ISBN: 978-1-4206-3539-3

© 2015 Teacher Created Resources
Made in U.S.A.

Teacher Created Resources

TABLE OF CONTENTS

TABLE OF CONTENTS (cont.)

CONNECTING WITH THE COMMON CORE

This book responds to the Common Core State Standards' goals of helping students develop the skills necessary to be successful in college and career. Through focused analysis, comparison, and synthesis of two texts, students will strengthen their understanding of literary conventions and build on analytical and argumentation skills. The texts selected for this book represent the high-quality, complex, and engaging new literature that is being produced in today's middle-grade publishing. These contemporary titles are easily relatable to the 21st-century child's experiences and knowledge, creating deeper connections between reader and text and giving the young reader a sense of ownership over the material.

The Common Core State Standards call for emphasis on assignments that encourage students to think critically, analyze deeply, and cite extensively from texts. Under the Common Core Standards, students are expected to progress in their level of comprehension and acquire appropriate academic vocabulary. In addition to building their reading and writing skills, students must also develop their listening and speaking skills in ways that will prepare them for the academic rigor of college.

To increase college readiness, Language Arts assignments are moving away from personal response and toward critical analysis based on information from texts. To prepare for the work they will encounter in college, students must become skilled at developing a strong claim and defending it with evidence from texts. To that end, *Using Paired Novels to Build Close Reading Skills* provides students with opportunities to interact with reading material deeply and in a variety of ways. Comparison activities strengthen students' understanding of the novels themselves, as well as the craft of writing. These activities

> The activities in this resource focus on two specific novels— *A Long Walk to Water* and *Home of the Brave*—but this same approach can be similarly applied when analyzing and comparing literature in general.

prompt students to examine how each author approaches literary elements such as characterization, theme, and point of view, and to draw conclusions based on the similarities or differences. In order to complete the tasks in these activities, students will need to reflect on their understanding of one book before making connections to the other—a process that will naturally support comprehension skills. The activities in this resource focus on two specific novels—*A Long Walk to Water* and *Home of the Brave*—but this same approach can be similarly applied when analyzing and comparing literature in general.

The activities in this book provide opportunities for individual and collaborative experiences. The individual activities build reading and writing skills by prompting students to develop analytical arguments and cite evidence from the texts. The collaborative activities help students develop critical speaking and listening skills in the context of literary analysis.

Ultimately, we want our children to develop a love of books and to become life-long readers. They can and should be encouraged to make personal connections to the texts and express their feelings about the stories they read. In fact, these types of connections often form the starting point for activities with more academic rigor. To provide students with freedom to interact with texts in more personal and creative ways, we have included Interactive Literature Notebook assignments as well as creative collaborative activities that are intended to enrich the reading experience and foster deeper personal enjoyment of the novels while still providing the foundation for deeper critical engagement.

HOW TO USE THIS BOOK

Section I (Units 1–6)

The purpose of this book is to provide you with a variety of activities that connect the two novels in ways that will foster deeper critical and analytical thinking in your students. Section I contains worksheets to be completed after both novels have been read. This section is divided into five units, which are based on the following literary elements: **Characterization** (pages 8–16), **Plot** (pages 17–26), **Setting and Genre** (pages 27–34), **Theme** (pages 35–42), and **Craft and Structure** (pages 43–53). A culminating sixth unit (pages 54–63) contains longer writing assignments and projects.

Unit features include . . .

* ### Teacher Instructions

    The first page of each unit provides you with an overview of the concept, the relevance to student learning, and brief descriptions and suggestions for each activity in the unit.

* ### Quick Guide to the Concept

    The top portion of this page provides your students with an introduction to the literary concept around which the unit is built, along with a list of related vocabulary words. The bottom portion contains a list of suggestions for **Interactive Literature Notebook** entries. The Interactive Literature Notebook can be used to allow students to think creatively about the reading and make personal connections to the novels. Some of the ideas can apply to both books, while others are specific to one or the other novel. You can assign a specific topic to your students or allow them to pick from these suggestions. More detailed instructions for the Interactive Literature Notebook can be found on page 6.

* ### Unit Activities

    Each unit contains **individual** and **collaborative** activities that support your students' understanding of literary elements and author's craft. Most of the activities also emphasize the use of textual evidence in the form of summarizing, paraphrasing, or quoting. In addition, some are meant to be used as **linked** assignments, with one activity laying the foundation for the next. In some cases, a collaborative activity allows students to brainstorm ideas and discuss the books together before completing a more challenging task in an individual worksheet. Alternately, an individual activity may provide students with an opportunity to reflect on the reading and then practice listening, speaking, and paraphrasing skills in a linked collaborative activity. Look for the following icons in the upper-right corner of each activity page:

 = individual 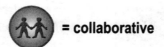 = collaborative  = linked

Section II (Units 7–9)

In this section, you will find activities to use during the reading of the individual books. These activities are divided into three groups: those that can be used with either novel, those intended to be used with *A Long Walk to Water*, and those intended to be used with *Home of the Brave*. These activities are meant to supplement the single-novel study activities you may already use. You may want to have students keep all of their single-novel worksheets in a folder and refer back to them when they are completing the novel-comparison activities. This will provide your students with opportunities to review the material, refresh their memories of the books, and practice using notes as a reference for a current assignment.

WHAT IS AN INTERACTIVE LITERATURE NOTEBOOK?

An Interactive Literature Notebook is a notebook that combines learning materials with personal response. For each student, his or her notebook will serve as a place to record and organize the information learned about the elements of literature. The response pages also encourage a deeper level of creativity and personal reflection toward the novels being analyzed and discussed in class.

For this resource, students may use a composition book, a spiral notebook, or a three-ring binder, depending on teacher preferences and needs. Instruct students to organize their notebooks as follows:

On the RIGHT side of the notebook:
Students record new information they are learning about literary elements and writer's craft.

On the LEFT side of the notebook:
Students create a personal-response page. This encourages students to process and apply the concepts in ways of their choosing.

TIP: Leave a blank page at the beginning and have students keep a table of contents as they go so they can easily find information in the future.

Interactive Literature Notebooks help your students hone the organizational skills they will need to be successful learners in high school and college by developing their competence in note-taking and record-keeping. These notebooks are excellent tools for visual as well as linguistic learners, and they give all students experience in connecting visual and multimedia components with text.

CONTEMPORARY CLASSICS

A Long Walk to Water
Linda Sue Park (2010)

A Long Walk to Water is a fictionalized story based on the life of a Sudanese Lost Boy, Salva Dut, who was forced to flee his village in 1985 when soldiers attacked. The narrative alternates between Salva's experience in 1985 and the story of a Sudanese girl in 2008 who must spend her days walking for hours to bring water to her family. Linda Sue Park draws from research and interviews with Salva Dut to create a heartbreaking fictionalized account of his harrowing journey. The majority of the action in the novel takes place in 1985–1986, making the genre historical fiction, albeit recent history. Although Nya's brief sections take place in 2008–2009, and Salva's story continues into 2009, the primary focus of the novel is the depiction of the horrors and struggles Salva faces on his journey to the refugee camps. The two narratives ultimately connect in an uplifting, hopeful ending that will inspire young readers.

Awards and Honors

➤ *New York Times* Best Seller
➤ IRA Notable Books for a Global Society 2011
➤ Jane Addams Children's Book Award 2011

Note: Page numbers in this guide refer to the 2010 paperback edition published by Houghton Mifflin Harcourt, Boston/ New York.

Home of the Brave
Katherine Applegate (2007)

This verse novel by Newbery Medal-winning author Katherine Applegate tells the story of a young Sudanese refugee, Kek, as he adapts to a new life in the United States. Kek is haunted by memories of the family and home he has lost, as well as the violence he witnessed. Yet he remains hopeful that he will one day reunite with his missing mother. Kek's amazement and misunderstandings of American life provide both bittersweet and humorous moments throughout the novel. He soon becomes the caretaker for a lonely old cow, who serves as a connection to and symbol of his old life and family. The first-person narration, as well as the poetic form, give readers insight into the emotions and thoughts of a refugee of war.

Awards and Honors

➤ *School Library Journal* Best Books of the Year 2007
➤ SCBWI Golden Kite Award for Best Fiction 2008
➤ Bank Street Josette Frank Award 2008

Note: Page numbers in this guide refer to the 2008 paperback edition published by Feiwel and Friends (an imprint of Macmillan Children's Publishing Group), New York.

UNIT 1 TEACHER INSTRUCTIONS

When students analyze *character*, they increase their comprehension of the author's craft and purpose, and they build their understanding of the way character development relates to theme. In this unit, your class will analyze how the authors reveal character and how the secondary characters contribute to the story. Students will make connections between the characters in both novels to strengthen their understanding of how characterization relates to theme. They will discuss and write about the ways the protagonists respond to challenges and draw conclusions based on evidence from the text.

Introduce students to the concept of characterization by distributing the top portion of "A Quick Guide to Characterization" (page 9). The bottom portion offers suggestions for using Interactive Notebooks to reinforce learning. Distribute any or all of these when appropriate.

Unit 1 includes the following components. See page 5 of this book for an explanation of icons.

"Getting to Know the Characters" (page 10) — Consider author's craft and examine the ways in which authors develop characters. Examine how the protagonists view themselves, how they act, and how others view them in the novel, as well as how each protagonist changes. (*TIP:* After students complete this worksheet individually, have them compare answers and use their ideas as a springboard for brainstorming personality traits in the next activity.)

"Alike and Different" (page 11) — Build discussion and collaboration skills by brainstorming a list of traits for each main character and drawing conclusions about the characters' similarities.

"Compare the Pair!" (page 12) — Use the ideas generated in group discussion to further analyze how these characters are similar. Provide textual support for responses.

"Helping Hands" (pages 13–14) — Complete a close reading of selected passages, summarize information, and analyze two important secondary characters. Make comparisons about the characters and their roles in the protagonists' success. (*TIP:* Use this worksheet for modeling close reading. Read the passage in *A Long Walk to Water* aloud and ask students questions to help them fill in the information. Then have them practice their skills by applying close-reading strategies to the *Home of the Brave* questions.)

"A Family of Friends" (page 15) — Read passages from both novels and find quotations about the protagonists' thoughts on family. Next, explain the importance of a quotation from one character in *A Long Walk to Water* and apply the concept to characters in both novels.

"Two Tribes" (page 16) — Understand characterization as it relates to author's purpose. Identify characters' attitudes about the Nuer and Dinka tribes and analyze how the authors' characterizations help readers gain a better understanding. (*TIP:* Guide students and help them recognize that without Nya, readers may assume the Nuer are cruel and violent, based on Salva's fears and experience. However, as part of the Nuer tribe, Nya has the same fears about the Dinka. Also, Kek's family is Nuer. These characters help readers understand that the conflict between the two tribes is not a matter of good guys and bad guys.)

A QUICK GUIDE TO CHARACTERIZATION

Great stories need great *characters*. Characters are the people or animals in a story. The author helps us get to know the characters through *characterization*. This is the process of giving readers clues that help us understand who the characters are and why they are important to the story.

Unit Vocabulary
- ✓ characters
- ✓ characterization
- ✓ protagonist
- ✓ antagonist
- ✓ secondary characters
- ✓ dynamic character
- ✓ static character

✳ What does the character say?

✳ How does the character act?

✳ What does the character look like?

✳ What do other characters say about him or her?

✳ How do other characters react to him or her?

The *protagonist* is the main character of the story.

The *antagonist* is the person or force that is against the main character.

Secondary characters are characters who are important but are not the main focus of the story. They help move the plot along and help us understand the main character.

A character that changes by the end of the novel is called a *dynamic* character.

Characters that stay the same throughout the novel are called *static* characters.

INTERACTIVE LITERATURE NOTEBOOK SUGGESTIONS FOR UNIT 1

1 Character Collage	2 Character Growth	3 Questions for Nya	4 Being a Leader	5 Hannah's Letter
Use pictures and words to create a character collage that represents the protagonist of one of the novels. In the middle of the page, write down a quote that represents the main character.	After reading a few chapters of the novel, stop and think about the main character. How do you think that character will change by the end of the book? Why do you think this?	*A Long Walk to Water* is based on a true story of Salva Dut, but Nya is a fictional character. Imagine Nya is a real girl. Write five questions you would like to ask her about her life in Sudan, both before the well was built in her village and after.	What qualities are important in a good leader? Create a page that highlights three of the most important qualities. Explain why you think they are necessary for leadership. Add pictures or names of people and/or fictional characters that exhibit all three of these qualities.	In *Home of the Brave*, Kek convinces Hannah to write a short letter to her mom. What do you think that letter said? Imagine you are Hannah and write the letter. Then explain what this letter shows us about Hannah.

Name: _____

GETTING TO KNOW THE CHARACTERS

Look closely at how the authors help us get to know the main characters. Use evidence from the novels to support your answers.

	Salva	Kek
How do the protagonists describe themselves?		
Quotation to support answer		
How do the protagonists act at the beginning of the novel?		
Quotation to support answer		
How do other characters view the protagonists at the beginning?		
Quotation to support answer		
How do the protagonists act at the end of the novel?		
Quotation to support answer		
How do other people view them at the end?		
Quotation to support answer		

Name(s): _____

ALIKE AND DIFFERENT

With a partner or small group, brainstorm a list of traits that describe the protagonist of each novel. Discuss which traits they have in common. Decide which traits your group thinks are most important and why.

Words that describe Salva   **Words that describe both**   **Words that describe Kek**

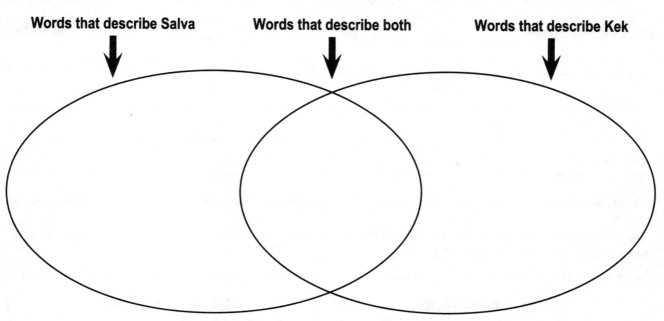

1. Are their personalities more alike or different? Explain.

_____

_____

_____

2. Which personality trait does your group think was most important for each boy?

	Kek	**Salva**
Trait		
Does the other boy also have this trait?		
Why is this trait most important for this character?		
Give an example of how having this trait helped this character.		

COMPARE THE PAIR!

Now that you have discussed both characters with your group, think about the traits Kek and Salva have in common. Pick one trait to write about.

Salva and Kek are both _____ because they

_____

_____

_____

_____

Use evidence from the books to support your point. Summarize a scene or use a quotation that shows this trait in each character.

A Long Walk to Water	*Home of the Brave*
Scene: _____	Scene: _____
_____	_____
_____	_____
Summary or quotation: _____	Summary or quotation: _____
_____	_____
_____	_____
_____	_____
_____	_____
_____	_____
_____	_____
_____	_____
Page number: _____	Page number: _____

Name: _____

HELPING HANDS

Both novels have secondary characters that help change the protagonists' lives. Salva and Kek both develop important friendships with refugee aid workers. Examine the influence these men had on the main characters.

> ## A Long Walk to Water

Salva spends all of his teen years in refugee camps in Africa. When he is 22, he meets an aid worker named Michael at the Ifo camp in Kenya. Review Chapter Fourteen. Michael has only a small part in this novel, but he has a significant impact on Salva's life.

1. How is Michael different from the other aid workers Salva has met?

_____

_____

Find a quotation that supports your answer and write it here.

_____

_____

2. What important things did Michael teach Salva?

_____

_____

3. Why do you think Michael took such an interest in Salva? What did he see in Salva that was special?

_____

_____

Find a quotation that supports your answer and write it here.

_____

_____

4. Based on the information provided about Michael, what can you infer about the kind of person he is? Explain how you can infer this.

_____

_____

5. Why was meeting Michael important for preparing Salva for life in the United States?

_____

_____

HELPING HANDS (cont.)

Home of the Brave

Unlike Salva and Michael, Dave and Kek meet in the United States and know each other longer. Dave is also an English-speaking aid worker. He has a bigger part in the novel than Michael does in *A Long Walk to Water*, but the two men are similar in several ways.

6. Read the poem "What the Heck" (pages 11–12). What does Kek refer to Dave as?

_____

Quote the line here: _____

_____

7. Dave works for the Refugee Resettlement Center. Think about Dave's role in the novel and his interactions with Kek, his family, and his teachers. How would you describe Dave's job?

_____

_____

8. Skim through the novel and list several specific things Dave does to help Kek and his family.

_____

_____

_____

PUTTING IT ALL TOGETHER

9. How are Dave and Michael similar in their personalities? _____

_____

_____

10. Dave and Michael meet Kek and Salva through their work at refugee aid organizations. Do you think Dave and Michael see their relationships with Kek and Salva as just part of their job? Explain your answer.

_____

_____

_____

11. Do you think these men did more for Kek and Salva than their jobs required? Explain.

_____

_____

UNIT 1: CHARACTERIZATION

Name: _____

A FAMILY OF FRIENDS

At the beginning of both novels, Salva and Kek have been separated from their families. Look through the following chapters for quotations that show these characters' thoughts about their families. For each quotation, provide the page numbers.

A Long Walk to Water
Chapter Two (pages 8–13)
Chapter Three (pages 14–19)

Home of the Brave
"Questions" (pages 8–9)
"TV Machine" (pages 39–42)

1. How are Salva and Kek's thoughts similar?

_____

_____

2. Look back at the conversation Salva and Uncle have on page 60 of *A Long Walk to Water*. Why is Salva upset that his uncle wants to return to Sudan to fight?

_____

_____

3. What does Uncle tell him about the idea of "family"?

_____

_____

Salva and Kek both move to the United States. How do the people they meet in America become a new kind of family, like Uncle suggests? Give examples of something the American friends do to show they are like a family to the boys.

Novel	A Long Walk to Water	Home of the Brave
Friends	Chris and Louise	Hannah
What They Do		

4. How do these friendships help Salva and Kek?

_____

_____

_____

Name: _____

TWO TRIBES

Review Salva's section in Chapter Three of *A Long Walk to Water* ("Southern Sudan, 1985").

1. How does Salva feel when he sees the Dinka scars on the old woman at the farm?

_____

_____

2. How does he feel about the Nuer tribe? _____

List words or phrases that show how he feels. _____

3. At the end of this chapter, Salva is relieved to see more people from the Dinka tribe. What does the Dinka ritual scar on the forehead look like?

_____

_____

Review Nya's section in Chapter Six of *A Long Walk to Water* ("Southern Sudan, 2008").

4. Nya is from the Nuer tribe. In Chapter Six, Nya realizes why her mother hates going to the lake camp. What is the main reason her mother hates the camp?

_____

Find a quotation to support your answer and write it here: _____

_____

5. How would you describe Nya and her family? _____

_____

6. Why do you think the author made Nya a Nuer instead of a Dinka?

_____

7. In *Home of the Brave*, the author never mentions tribe names, but Kek describes Ganwar's scars as six long lines across his forehead. Based on the description of the scars, what tribe are Kek and Ganwar from?

_____

8. How would you describe Kek and his family? _____

_____

9. If you had read only Salva's story, without Nya's character in it, how do you think you would have felt about the Nuer tribe?

_____

_____

10. How are Salva, Nya, Kek, and their families similar? _____

_____

UNIT 2 TEACHER INSTRUCTIONS

The *plot* is the series of events that make up the action of the novel. It is what *happens* in the story. The *conflict*, the problem at the heart of the story, is an essential part of the plot. A chronological plot describes events in the order they happen and usually follows a traditional structure: Exposition, Rising Action, Climax, Falling Action, and Resolution.

In this unit, students will analyze plot structure, conflict, and resolution. They will compare how the characters deal with conflicts, and they will draw conclusions about the similarities and differences in the plots of these novels. Students will use critical and creative thinking to articulate their understanding of plot structure.

Introduce students to the concept of plot by distributing the top portion of "A Quick Guide to Plot" (page 18) and "A Quick Guide to Plot Structure" (page 19). The bottom portion of page 18 offers suggestions for using Interactive Notebooks to reinforce learning. Distribute any or all of these when appropriate.

Unit 2 includes the following components. See page 5 of this book for an explanation of icons.

 "Types of Conflict" (page 20) — Consider how three common types of conflict appear in each novel. After identifying examples of each conflict, determine which type of conflict is the most significant in the story.

 "Taking the Conflict Further" (page 21) — Build on the ideas generated in the "Types of Conflict" worksheet. As members of a team, discuss ideas and elaborate on further points. (*TIP:* Assign students to groups of three to four members.)

 "Plotting Problems" (page 22) — Identify three significant plot points that help the characters grow. After identifying examples of major struggles in each novel, discuss the similarities and differences in the ways the characters respond to difficult situations.

 "Turning Points" (page 23) — Read significant sections of the books to understand how major plot points affect the story as a whole. (*TIP:* Consider reading these sections aloud and having students summarize afterwards.)

 "Talking About Turning Points" (page 24) — This activity draws upon the work done in the previous worksheet. Practice listening and speaking by taking notes on partners' summaries and furthering the discussion.

 "Resolution" (page 25) — Examine the resolution to each novel, summarize, make comparisons, and draw conclusions based on opinions.

 "Starting Over" (page 26) — Compare how the concept of assimilation to life in the United States is a major similarity in both plots. Work together in small groups to brainstorm lists and then draw a conclusion about which character will have an easier time adjusting to American life.

A QUICK GUIDE TO PLOT

The *plot* is what happens in the story. It is made up of the events that take place in a specific *sequence* in the book, from the **beginning** to the **middle** to the **end**.

The *conflict* is the main problem in the story. There are several types of conflicts, including the following:

❋ **Person vs. Person** — The main character struggles with another person or people in the story.

❋ **Person vs. Self** — The main character struggles with emotions, thoughts, or feelings that create the problems in the story.

❋ **Person vs. Nature** — The main character struggles with something in nature, such as the wilderness or a big storm.

❋ **Person vs. Society** — The main character struggles against the beliefs, behaviors, or traditions of society.

Unit Vocabulary

✓ plot
✓ sequence
✓ conflict
✓ exposition
✓ climax
✓ resolution

INTERACTIVE LITERATURE NOTEBOOK SUGGESTIONS FOR UNIT 2

1 In Five Years	2 Filmstrip	3 An Important Scene	4 Someplace New	5 Tweet It!
Predict the fictional future: based on the events in the story, what do you think will happen to the characters after the end of the novel? Write a paragraph imagining the characters five years later.	Create a filmstrip of several major events in the story.	Find or create pictures that represent one of the most important scenes in the story. Write a one-sentence summary of the scene and an explanation about why you chose it.	If you have ever moved to a new place, write about your experience. Even if you did not move to a new country, what changes did you have to adjust to?	In 140 characters or less, explain what this book is about.

A QUICK GUIDE TO PLOT STRUCTURE

Many novels follow a classic plot structure. They first introduce characters, and then they introduce conflict into the lives of those characters. Characters struggle with this conflict (or conflicts) until a turning point occurs. By the end of the novel, this conflict is resolved.

The following diagram shows this structure. Each point on the diagram is explained below.

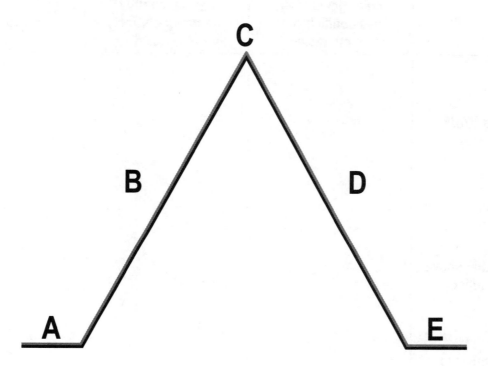

A. Exposition – the information and events that set up the story and introduce characters

B. Rising Action – the series of events that build excitement or tension by showing the characters struggling with the conflict

C. Climax – the most tense or exciting part of the story and the turning point when we begin to see how the conflict might end

D. Falling Action – the events that show what happens to the characters after the conflict is resolved or is beginning to be resolved

E. Resolution – the ending

Name: _____

TYPES OF CONFLICT

The *conflict* of the story is the problem the main character faces. Most stories have more than one conflict. Complete the chart to show how three different types of conflict are presented in the novels.

	Person vs. Society How do attitudes or behaviors of the culture and/or government cause conflict for the main characters?	**Person vs. Person** How does the protagonist struggle against another character or characters in the novel?	**Person vs. Self** What thoughts, behaviors, or emotions does the main character struggle to overcome?
A Long Walk to Water			
Quotation that shows this conflict:			
Page number(s):			
Home of the Brave			
Quotation that shows this conflict:			
Page number(s):			

Name(s): _____

TAKING THE CONFLICT FURTHER

With your group, share your chart from the "Types of Conflict" worksheet. Each person in the group should share at least one conflict and example. When one person is talking, the rest of the group should listen carefully.

1. Were everyone's answers more similar or different?

	More Similar	**More Different**
A Long Walk to Water		
➤ Person vs. Society	○	○
➤ Person vs. Person	○	○
➤ Person vs. Self	○	○
Home of the Brave		
➤ Person vs. Society	○	○
➤ Person vs. Person	○	○
➤ Person vs. Self	○	○

2. Which type of conflict does your group think is the most important conflict for Salva?

_____

Why? _____

_____

_____

3. Which type of conflict does your group think is the most important conflict for Kek?

_____

Why? _____

_____

_____

4. Did your group pick the same conflict for both answers? ❑ **Yes** ❑ **No**

Why do you think your answers were the same or different?

_____

_____

_____

Name(s): _____

PLOTTING PROBLEMS

The plots of both novels include many difficult and even traumatic situations Kek and Salva face. How do the characters react to these situations? Think about how these struggles affect the choices the characters make. Find three examples of difficult situations the characters face in each novel. Discuss how the character reacts to each situation.

	Salva	Kek
Situation #1		
Reaction		
Page numbers		
Situation #2		
Reaction		
Page numbers		
Situation #3		
Reaction		
Page numbers		

Answer the following questions about how these characters react to situations.

1. Explain one way Salva and Kek's reactions to difficult circumstances are similar.

_____

_____

_____

2. Explain one way Salva and Kek respond differently to difficult circumstances.

_____

_____

_____

TURNING POINTS

Review Salva's section of Chapter Thirteen in *A Long Walk to Water* (pages 77–82).

1. Summarize what happens in this chapter.

_____

_____

_____

_____

_____

2. Find a quotation that shows Salva is a good leader:

_____

_____

_____

Now reread "Running Away" and "Bus" (pages 204–209) in *Home of the Brave*.

3. Summarize what happens in these poems.

_____

_____

_____

_____

_____

4. In "Running Away" (page 204), Kek says the following:

> "I want to be in a place where the things
> I love and know
> Are there within my reach"

From these two poems, find a quotation that shows Kek *has* found some things in the U.S. that he loves and knows, even if he doesn't realize it when he first runs away.

_____

_____

_____

- -

Name(s): _____

TALKING ABOUT TURNING POINTS

You have just summarized important scenes in *A Long Walk to Water* and *Home of the Brave*. Work with a partner to discuss your summaries and answer questions about these passages. One partner will read his or her summary for the chapter in *A Long Walk to Water* while the other partner listens and writes down notes. Then you will switch roles for *Home of the Brave*.

	A Long Walk to Water	Home of the Brave
Speaker's Name		
Listener's Name		
Listener's Notes ➤ What I liked ➤ What is missing ➤ What is confusing		

Now discuss the following questions and write down your answers.

1. What events happened earlier in *A Long Walk to Water* that helped Salva know what to do and how to help the other boys in this scene?

   _____

   _____

2. Throughout most of *Home of the Brave*, Kek seems hopeful. Why do you think he loses hope at this point in the story? Was it one incident or several things? Explain.

   _____

   _____

3. How are Kek's and Salva's actions and thoughts similar in these sections?

   _____

   _____

4. How are Kek's and Salva's actions and thoughts different in these sections?

   _____

   _____

   _____

24

Name: _____

RESOLUTION

The ending of a book should follow logically from the sequence of events in the story. Reread the last chapters of each book and answer the questions below.

	A Long Walk to Water	Home of the Brave
In your own words, explain what happens at the end of the novel.		
Did it end the way you expected it to? Explain why or why not.		
What is your opinion of the way the book ends?		

1. In what ways are the endings similar in these books?

   _____

   _____

2. In what ways are the endings different?

   _____

   _____

3. Which ending did you like better?

   ❏ *A Long Walk to Water*   ❏ *Home of the Brave*

4. Explain your answer to question #3.

   _____

   _____

   _____

STARTING OVER

Salva and Kek are both refugees from Sudan who immigrated to the United States to start a new life. The plot of *Home of the Brave* starts as Kek arrives in America, but the plot of *A Long Walk to Water* is coming to an end when Salva immigrates to the U.S. Even though the move to the United States happens at very different times in the plots, both novels show the difficulty of adjusting to a new culture.

> **"The freedom is a great gift,**
>
> **she says. To choose your leaders.**
>
> **To walk the streets unafraid.**
>
> **But it's lonely here.**
>
> **And . . . she hesitates. Hard."**
>
> — Kek's aunt
> Discussing her new life in the U.S.
> *Home of the Brave* (page 90)

1. Other than freedom, what do Kek and Salva have in the United States that they did not have in Sudan? Work together to brainstorm a list.

   _____

   _____

   _____

2. Even though life in the U.S. has many advantages, it is very different from the life Kek and Salva are used to and the culture in which they grew up. What do Kek and Salva miss about their lives in Sudan? Work together to brainstorm a list.

   _____

   _____

   _____

3. Kek is 11 when he moves to the U.S. Salva is 22. Who do you think will have more difficulty getting used to a new culture and way of life? Explain your answer.

   _____

   _____

   _____

- -

UNIT 3 TEACHER INSTRUCTIONS

The *setting* of a novel is an important element to examine. Students should be able to identify not just the *time* and *place* of the story, but also how those details influence characters and drive plot. Readers should be asked to examine how the environment affects the people and events in the story. Additionally, students can analyze the writer's craft by identifying how the author uses details and description to create a vivid environment.

Setting is also an essential part of identifying the *genre* of each of these novels: *historical fiction* and *contemporary realistic fiction*. In this unit, students will examine how setting relates to genre in historical and contemporary realistic fiction. By looking closely at how time period affects story and comparing how these different genres are crafted, readers will gain a deeper understanding of differences in genre and its relationship to the writer's purpose.

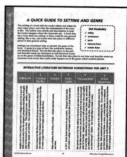

Introduce students to the concepts of setting and genre by distributing the top portion of "A Quick Guide to Setting and Genre" (page 28). The bottom portion offers suggestions for using Interactive Notebooks to reinforce learning. Distribute any or all of these when appropriate.

Unit 3 includes the following components. See page 5 of this book for an explanation of icons.

 "A Sense of Place" (page 29) — Read closely to identify, explain, and compare the authors' use of descriptive words and sensory details to create a vivid environment.

 "The Past and the Present" (page 30) — Work together to identify details in each story that relate to historical events.

 "School Days" (page 31) — Review passages in each novel and create paragraph descriptions of the way schools are described in each book.

 "Setting and Meaning" (page 32) — Examine how authors use setting to represent more than just environment. Compare Kek's and Salva's reactions to the weather when they first land in America.

 "Discussing Setting and Meaning" (page 33) — With partners, take turns answering questions about the way setting influences mood, serves as a symbol, and foreshadows future experiences. Listeners paraphrase and respond to speakers, then switch roles.

 "A Deeper Understanding of Setting" (page 34) — Reflect on how the reading of one novel influenced the experience of reading the other. (*TIP:* These novels are both based on real-world situations, and reading one book gives readers prior knowledge and deeper understanding as they read the second book. *A Long Walk to Water*'s final chapters describe Salva's immigration to the United Sates, and *Home of the Brave* begins just as Kek arrives in the U.S. Each book offers readers additional insight into gaps in the other narrative.)

A QUICK GUIDE TO SETTING AND GENRE

The *setting* of a book tells the reader **where** and **when** the story takes place and what the *environment* of the story is like. The author uses details and descriptions to help the reader imagine where the characters are. A book may have more than one setting; or there could be one general setting, like a city, and scenes that take place in different locations within that general setting.

Settings can sometimes help us identify the *genre* of the book. A genre—such as nonfiction, fantasy, or historical fiction—is a type of text. Novels that take place in the past and describe made-up characters in real historical events are in the genre of *historical fiction*. Novels that take place in our time and describe made-up characters and events that could really happen are in the genre called *realistic fiction*.

Unit Vocabulary

✓ setting

✓ environment

✓ genre

✓ historical fiction

✓ realistic fiction

INTERACTIVE LITERATURE NOTEBOOK SUGGESTIONS FOR UNIT 3

1 A New Life	2 Crossing the Nile	3 Timeline	4 South Sudan	5 The Long Walk	6 A New Experience
Imagine one of the Lost Boys came from a refugee camp to live in your city. Write a journal entry from the refugee's perspective describing his thoughts when he first arrived in your town. Think about your town—weather, landscape, buildings, people, and activities. How would the newcomer react?	Salva crosses the Nile River in boats the group spends two days making. Use information from Chapters 8 and 9, as well as research about the Nile, to create a page of facts and images about the Nile River.	Make a timeline of the history of Sudan. Include important events and dates.	In 2011, South Sudan became its own country. Research South Sudan and create a collage of images and facts about life in South Sudan today.	Nya spends most of her day walking to the pond to get water for her family. One trip takes several hours, and she must go twice a day to bring enough water for the family. Imagine you have to walk across your city to get supplies for your family. Describe what you would see, hear, touch, taste, and smell as you walked from one end of your city to the other. What types of places would you pass through? (Option: Use Google Maps to create a route.)	In *Home of the Brave*, Kek goes to the mall and the grocery store for the first time. Both experiences are overwhelming for him. Go to a public place you have been to many times—a store, a movie theater, or a restaurant. Imagine what Kek would experience walking into this place for the first time. Write a paragraph describing this place through Kek's eyes.

Name: _____

A SENSE OF PLACE

Authors use descriptive language to make the setting come to life. Reread the passages listed here and find examples of words or phrases that help you understand the setting.

Find words and phrases that describe sensory images.

Novel	A Long Walk to Water	Home of the Brave
Passage	"Chapter Three, Southern Sudan, 1985"	"Working" and "Ganwar, Meet Gol"
Pages	pages 15–19	pages 136–141
Where does this passage take place?		
What is happening at this point in the story?		
List descriptive words and phrases that help you picture where the scene takes place. What details does the author use to help you imagine this place?		
What is the mood or feeling of this scene?		

1. What are the similarities in these two passages?

_____

_____

2. What are the differences in these two passages?

_____

_____

3. Which passage did you think was easiest to picture?

_____

4. What made that passage easier to picture than the other one?

_____

_____

THE PAST AND THE PRESENT

A Long Walk to Water and *Home of the Brave* are about similar topics, but one is historical fiction and one is contemporary fiction because of *when* most of the story takes place. Novels that take place in the past and portray real historical events in the storytelling are called *historical fiction*. Novels that take place in our current time are called *realistic fiction* or *contemporary realistic fiction*. With a partner or small group, discuss how these authors show the time period that is part of each book's setting.

Novel	A Long Walk to Water	Home of the Brave
Is most of the story set in the past or present?		
How much time passes from the beginning of the novel to the end?		
What real historical events are described in the novel?		
How are the lives of the characters affected by the real historical events?		
Find one quotation that shows how the main male character feels about these events.		
What is the mood or feeling of this scene?		

PUTTING IT ALL TOGETHER

Why is one book considered historical fiction and one contemporary fiction?

_____

_____

_____

SCHOOL DAYS

Classrooms and schools are important settings used in each of the novels. Compare and contrast the way these settings are used in the two novels.

1. Review Chapter One and Chapter Two of *A Long Walk to Water*. Write a description of what school is like for the children in Salva's village before the attack. Describe who goes to school, when they go, and what the classroom is like.

   _____

   _____

   _____

   _____

2. Now look at Kek's school experience in *Home of the Brave*. Review the poems on pages 66–78. Write a paragraph describing Kek's school in the United States. Describe who goes to school, what the whole school is like, and what Kek's class is like.

   _____

   _____

   _____

   _____

   _____

   _____

3. What do you think are the biggest differences in these types of schools?

   _____

   _____

   _____

4. At the end of *A Long Walk to Water*, Nya finds out her village will get a school. Reread pages 103–104. Write a paragraph describing how Nya feels about school and why you think she feels this way.

   _____

   _____

   _____

   _____

   _____

   _____

SETTING AND MEANING

Authors can use setting to help readers understand deeper meaning in a novel. Setting can help readers understand how the characters are feeling. It can also be used to foreshadow what will happen later in the novel.

1. What time of year do Kek and Salva arrive in the United States?

_____

Brainstorm a list of words that usually describe this season.

Look back at your list. Circle the words on your list that seem more negative.

2. Find quotations from both novels to show how Kek and Salva respond to the environment when they first arrive in the United States:

A Long Walk to Water pages 95–96	*Home of the Brave* pages 3, 4, and 8
_____	_____
_____	_____
_____	_____
_____	_____

3. How are Kek's reaction and Salva's reaction similar?

_____

_____

4. Why do you think they reacted the same way?

_____

_____

_____

Name(s): _____

DISCUSSING SETTING AND MEANING

Share your answers from the "Setting and Meaning" worksheet. Then each partner will take a turn giving an opinion while the other person listens, paraphrases, and responds.

After sharing your answers on "Setting and Meaning," discuss the *mood* of these scenes. What feeling or mood do you get from the way the setting is described in these passages? Each partner should answer this question and explain his/her answer.

Feeling or mood from *A Long Walk to Water* (pages 95–96): _____

_____

Explanation: _____

_____

_____

Feeling or mood from *Home of the Brave* (pages 3, 4, and 8): _____

_____

Explanation: _____

_____

_____

PRACTICE SPEAKING AND LISTENING!

Speaker 1: _____   **Speaker 2:** _____
                      (name)   *(name)*

Answer the following question aloud and support your opinion with examples from the novels. *How are the boys' reactions to the settings similar to their reactions to other experiences they have in America?*	Paraphrase your partner's answer. Then say whether you agree or disagree with your partner's opinion. Explain your opinion to your partner. ***then*** Answer the following question aloud and support your opinion with examples from the novels. *How does the weather in these scenes symbolize how the boys feel when they arrive in this new country compared to how they felt with their families in their old villages?*
Paraphrase your partner's answer. Then say whether you agree or disagree with your partner's opinion. Explain your opinion to your partner.	

Name: _____

A DEEPER UNDERSTANDING OF SETTING

Use the following prompts to dig deeper into the role that setting plays in each of these novels.

1. How did reading *A Long Walk to Water* help you understand more about Kek's past in *Home of the Brave*?

   _____

   _____

   _____

   _____

2. *A Long Walk to Water* is mostly about Salva's experiences walking hundreds of miles across Sudan to reach safety. Although he eventually comes to the United States, there are only a few paragraphs about his first six years in New York. How did reading *Home of the Brave* help you understand more about Salva's experience coming to the United States?

   _____

   _____

   _____

   _____

3. Which book did you read first? (Place a checkmark in the appropriate box.)

   ❑ *A Long Walk to Water*   ❑ *Home of the Brave*

4. Do you think this was a good order to read them in, or would you recommend reading the other book first? Explain your answer.

   _____

   _____

   _____

5. If someone wanted to read just one of the books, which one would you recommend? Explain your reasons.

   _____

   _____

   _____

   _____

UNIT 4 TEACHER INSTRUCTIONS

The *theme* is the main idea or message behind the story. Students should be guided to think about the significance of each novel and how characters, setting, and plot contribute to overall meaning. Consider what these books reveal about survival, immigration, friendship, courage, perseverance, and family.

In this unit, students will compare and contrast how these realistic novels treat similar themes. Students will conduct close readings of several passages in both novels to analyze and compare the way authors reveal themes through plot points and characters. Students will work together and individually to think deeply about major and minor themes that these novels share.

Introduce students to the concept of theme by distributing the top portion of "A Quick Guide to Theme" (page 36). The bottom portion offers suggestions for using Interactive Notebooks to reinforce learning. Distribute any or all of these when appropriate.

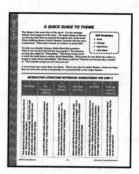

Unit 4 includes the following components. See page 5 of this book for an explanation of icons.

 "Theme Seeds" (page 37) — Work in small groups to compare how the same theme appears in both novels and to provide textual evidence. (*TIP:* Assign each theme listed on the handout to a group and have groups present their work to the class. As an option, consider beginning this activity with a whole-class discussion in which students identify the themes listed in the first section of the handout.)

 "Wisdom of Elders" (pages 38–39) — Perform close readings of two passages and analyze specific quotations. Identify the concept of taking something one step at a time and how this keeps a large task from becoming overwhelming. Consider the way this theme appears in both novels and draw conclusions about the authors' purpose.

 "A New World" (page 40) — Consider how each novel examines the immigrant experience of these Sudanese refugees. Begin by identifying struggles mentioned in *A Long Walk to Water*. Apply these struggles to those faced by Kek in *Home of the Brave*. (*TIP:* When naming new struggles that the refugees faced, students might list airplanes, paved roads, busy streets, fast cars, many white people, electricity, snow, the English language, reading, writing, etc.)

 "Discussing a New World" (page 41) — Work on listening and speaking skills by presenting ideas to partners, paraphrasing the other person's opinion, and responding with an opinion. Use this activity to synthesize ideas from both books and make an evaluation.

 "Gol" (page 42) — Understand the importance of cattle in Sudanese life and analyze how Gol represents the boys' old life in Sudan.

A QUICK GUIDE TO THEME

The *theme* is the main idea of the novel. It is the *message* behind what happens in the story. The *major theme* or themes are the big ideas that are present throughout the whole book. When thinking about a book's themes, consider *why* the story is important. What does it teach us or show us about life?

To help you identify themes, think about this question: *What are the big ideas that hold the story together?* For instance, one big idea might be "Friendship." The theme of the novel is what the book shows readers about friendship. What point do you think the author is trying to make about friendship? The theme could be "Friends can become like a family" or "True friends accept you for who you are."

A novel may have more than one theme. There may also be *minor themes*, which are ideas that are not in the novel as frequently or as prominently as the major themes.

> **Unit Vocabulary**
> ✓ theme
> ✓ message
> ✓ major theme
> ✓ minor theme

INTERACTIVE LITERATURE NOTEBOOK SUGGESTIONS FOR UNIT 4

1 One Word	2 The Importance of Water	3 Family Member	4 One Step at a Time	5 Interview	6 Working Hard to Improve
Think about how you would complete this sentence using only one word: This book makes me think about _____. Write this word in the middle of the page. Fill the rest of the page with pictures, words, and/or quotations that relate to this word. Be creative and artistic with your design.	*A Long Walk to Water* helps readers understand the importance of water in our lives. Create a page of water-conservation tips.	Pick one of your family members whom you admire. Write a description of the person and why you admire him or her. How has this person influenced you? Include a photograph.	Salva's uncle tells him to focus on one step at a time, and this advice helps Salva get through many years of struggles. Think of a situation you or someone you know has been in and explain how Uncle's advice would be helpful.	In *Home of the Brave*, Kek has a difficult time adjusting to his new life in America. Interview someone who has moved to the U.S. from another country to find out about his or her experience. Create a page for your questions and the person's answers.	Have you ever had to work very hard to get better at something? Describe what it was like to struggle to learn something. What did you do to get better at it?

THEME SEEDS

A Long Walk to Water and *Home of the Brave* have similar themes and ideas. A **theme** is the message behind the whole story. A novel could have several themes. For instance, here are some ideas that apply to both of these novels. Your group will select one of these topics and analyze how both books develop this theme.

What do the novels show readers about these topics?

- ▶ War
- ▶ Survival
- ▶ Family
- ▶ Hope
- ▶ Perseverance
- ▶ Immigration

Choose one of the above topics. Circle your choice and answer these questions.

1. What happens in *A Long Walk to Water* that shows this theme?

_____

_____

_____

Provide one quotation that supports your answer. (from page number: _____)

_____

_____

2. What happens in *Home of the Brave* that shows this theme?

_____

_____

_____

Provide one quotation that supports your answer. (from page number: _____)

_____

_____

3. How are these novels similar in the way they present this theme?

_____

_____

_____

4. How are the novels different in the way they present this theme?

_____

_____

_____

WISDOM OF ELDERS

In *A Long Walk to Water*, Salva's Uncle Jewiir helps Salva survive his long journey. Reread pages 52–54 and think about the important lesson Salva learns from his uncle.

1. Crossing the Akobo desert is very difficult for the entire group, and Salva almost gives up. What does Uncle Jewiir tell Salva to help him keep going? To support your answer, provide at least one quotation from the novel.

_____

_____

_____

_____

2. What does Uncle continue to do for the rest of the day?

_____

_____

3. What is the message or lesson in this advice?

_____

_____

_____

4. Why do you think this advice works for Salva in this situation?

_____

_____

_____

5. After Uncle Jewiir is killed, how does Salva continue to use this advice to survive?

_____

_____

_____

Find a quotation that shows this idea. (from page number: _____)

_____

_____

UNIT 4: THEME

WISDOM OF ELDERS (cont.)

Now look at the poem in *Home of the Brave* called "Ganwar" on pages 213–217.

6. How is Kek's attitude at the beginning of this poem similar to Salva's attitude during the Akobo walk?

_____

_____

7. Why does Kek feel this way? _____

_____

Find a quotation that shows this idea. (from page number: _____)

_____

_____

8. On page 216, near the end of this poem, Kek thinks,

"I remember something my mama
Used to say on dark days:
If you can talk, you can sing.
If you can walk, you can dance."

How is this idea similar to Uncle Jewiir's advice?

_____

_____

9. Give one example of Kek's actions that show this idea.

_____

_____

10. How important do you think these ideas are to Kek's and Salva's stories? Explain.

_____

_____

_____

Name: _____

A NEW WORLD

Life in the United States is very different from life in the villages of South Sudan. These novels help readers understand the difficulties refugees face as they try to adapt to a completely new way of life.

A Long Walk to Water takes place mostly in Sudan. At the end of the novel, Salva is chosen to come to the United States and live with an American family. The author does not give very many details about Salva's experience in the United States. Instead, she gives readers a brief explanation of some of the things Salva experienced when he first came to the U.S.

Read the passage on pages 97–99 about Salva's first month living in New York. List four things about the United States that were surprising or difficult for Salva.

1. _____

2. _____

3. _____

4. _____

Home of the Brave begins just as Kek arrives in the United States. Kek experiences some of the same confusion and difficulties that Salva did when he first arrived. The author of this book, however, describes Kek's experiences in great detail. Pick two of the answers you gave above and explain what Kek experienced. Use a quote to support each answer.

Answer from the list above: _____

What Kek experienced: _____

_____

Quotation that supports this answer: _____

_____

Page number: _____

Answer from the list above: _____

What Kek experienced: _____

_____

Quotation that supports this answer: _____

_____

Page number: _____

DISCUSSING A NEW WORLD

With a partner, share your answers from the "A New World" worksheet. Then take turns giving opinions while the other person listens, paraphrases, and responds.

Begin by deciding the order in which each partner will speak.

Speaker 1's Name: _____   **Speaker 2's Name:** _____

Speaker 1

Answer the following question aloud. Give reasons to support your answer.

➤ Who do you think had a more difficult time adjusting to life in the United States, Kek or Salva?

Speaker 2

➤ Paraphrase your partner's answer to the previous question.

➤ Do you agree or disagree with your partner's opinion? Explain your answer to your partner.

Now switch roles.

Speaker 2

Answer the following question aloud. Give reasons to support your answer.

➤ The real Salva Dut moved back to Sudan in 2011. After living in the United States, what do you think would be the most difficult part of moving back to Sudan?

Speaker 1

➤ Paraphrase your partner's answer to the previous question.

➤ Do you agree or disagree with your partner's opinion? Explain your answer to your partner.

TIME TO WORK TOGETHER!

The passage in *A Long Walk to Water* also says that Salva's new family helped him learn "the millions of things he had to learn" (page 98). Work together to think of two examples of things Kek experienced that Salva probably had to learn about, too, but that are not mentioned in *A Long Walk to Water*.

1. _____

   _____

2. _____

   _____

GOL

In *Home of the Brave*, Kek becomes the caretaker of a cow that he names Gol. Not only is this cow important in Kek's life, it also is a symbol of bigger ideas in both novels.

1. Why are cattle important in the everyday lives of the Sudanese people?

_____

_____

2. Scan the passages listed in the chart below. Find quotations from both novels to show how cows are important to the villagers of Sudan.

Novel	A Long Walk to Water	Home of the Brave
Passage	"Chapter One, Southern Sudan, 1985"	"God with a Wet Nose" and "Father"
Pages	1–7	13–16, 29–31
Quotation		

3. Kek takes care of a cow and names it "Gol." What does the word "Gol" mean?

_____

4. Why does Kek name the cow "Gol"? What does the cow represent for him?

_____

_____

5. How does Gol help Kek connect his old life to his new one?

_____

_____

_____

6. Kek, Ganwar, and Salva must all learn to adjust to American ways of life. Why is it important for them to continue to remember their native country and culture?

_____

_____

_____

UNIT 5 TEACHER INSTRUCTIONS

Examining writer's *craft* requires students to consider the author's intentions and how writing choices suit the purpose or artistry of a story. Many of the activities in the previous units and in the single-novel units (pages 64–92) address writer's craft in the context of literary elements. This section offers additional activities to further develop your students' understanding of the way authors craft stories.

In this unit, students will examine each novel's overall structure, paying attention to both authors' use of dividing the novels into sections and chapters. Students will also consider the use of African proverbs as an organizational tool; and they will analyze word choice as it relates to tone, consider the effectiveness of point of view, and compare poetry to prose.

Introduce students to the concepts of craft and structure by distributing "A Quick Guide to Craft and Structure" (pages 44–45). The bottom portion of page 45 offers suggestions for using Interactive Notebooks to reinforce learning. Distribute any or all of these when appropriate.

Unit 5 includes the following components. See page 5 of this book for an explanation of icons.

 "African Proverbs" (pages 46–47) — Examine the choices these authors made when organizing their texts. Look at Katherine Applegate's inclusion of African proverbs in *Home of the Brave* to provide a focal point for each section. Discuss each proverb's meaning and consider the relevance of these proverbs to the events in that particular section of the novel. Build on the understanding of the similarities in the novels by applying the proverbs to the events in Salva's and Nya's stories, as well.

 "Studying Writer's Craft" (page 48) — Continue studying the way authors structure stories by examining two elements used in both novels. Find examples of flashbacks and suspense-building techniques in both novels, explain their use, and evaluate their importance to the storytelling. (*TIP:* Before students begin this worksheet, have a class discussion about flashbacks and suspense. Have students provide explanations and write them on the board. You may also want to provide examples of flashback and cliffhangers from other novels or from video clips.)

 "Whose Point of View?" (page 49) — Think critically about the way point of view affects story. Recognize how Nya's sections in *A Long Walk to Water* make the result of Salva's journey more impactful.

 "What's Left Unsaid" (page 50) — Consider the authors' use of implied meaning by reading passages from both novels, summarizing explicit meaning, making inferences, and justifying assumptions.

 "Identifying Tone" (page 51) — Examine the way words and phrases contribute to the tone of a story or scene by identifying language that reflects tone in two passages. Apply understanding by selecting a passage to analyze. (*TIP:* Have each partner read one of the passages aloud to practice listening and speaking skills. For the final section, have each partner look through one book to find an example and then discuss which one to use on the worksheet.)

 "Form Flip" (pages 52–53) — Consider poetry and prose forms, what each style contributes to the overall work, and how the novels would change if written in a different form. Perform a close reading of two passages and identify quotes that demonstrate strong poetic and prosaic writing. Then rewrite these same passages as prose and poetry, and assess how effective the novels would be in that form. (*TIP:* Have students share their answers on the first page of the worksheet before moving on to the second. Discuss the qualities of poetry versus prose.)

A QUICK GUIDE TO CRAFT AND STRUCTURE

When writing a book, an author must make many choices. These choices affect the meaning and style of the book, and they greatly influence the readers' experience.

Forms of Writing

Literature comes in a variety of forms, such as prose, poetry, or drama. A novel written in *prose* uses sentences and paragraphs to express ideas. Prose writing sounds similar to the way we speak. *Poetry* uses creative line breaks, stanzas, and vivid language to express feelings, emotions, and images in fewer words than prose. Free-verse poetry is a type of poetry that does not use a specific pattern of rhyme or meter. Novels written in free-verse poetry still contain the same parts of the story (plot, character, theme), but the writing is more compact and does not sound like the way we normally speak.

Organization and Structure

Authors use various methods of organizing their novels, from small units like **paragraphs** or **stanzas**, to larger units like **chapters**, **sections**, or **parts.** Consider how the book is divided and other choices the author made in organizing the novel. If an author divides a novel into sections, think about what defines each section. How are the chapters in one section all related, and how are they different from the next section? Also, if each chapter has its own title, how does each title relate to the chapter? Also think about chapter length? How does the length of the chapter affect the pace of the story?

Unit Vocabulary

✓ prose
✓ poetry
✓ structure
✓ suspense
✓ cliffhanger
✓ foreshadowing
✓ flashback
✓ tone
✓ mood
✓ inference
✓ meaning
✓ literal (explicit)
✓ inferred (implied)
✓ point of view
✓ omniscient
✓ limited

Some authors use organization and structure to build *suspense*. An author may choose to end a chapter at a dramatic moment so readers are anxious to find out what happened. This type of *cliffhanger* leaves the reader wondering what will happen next. Authors may choose to use *foreshadowing* to hint at events to come. *Flashbacks* are sometimes used to reveal past events in order to give readers a better understanding of the characters and current situation. Another choice authors may make in structuring a novel is to *alternate* between two or more characters or narrators to give readers multiple perspectives of the events.

Tone and Mood

The author uses word choice, setting, and details to create the *tone* and *mood* of a story or scene. The author's *tone* shows the reader how the author or the narrator feels about the subject. This tone helps create the *mood* of the scene. *Mood* is the way the writing makes the reader feel.

Inference

When you read, the text can have a *literal* meaning and an *inferred* meaning. *Literal* or *explicit* meaning is what the passage actually says. The words directly state information. *Implied* or *inferred* meaning is information that is not stated directly in the text but can still be understood due to our previous knowledge and to clues provided in the text. This logical conclusion is called an *inference*.

A QUICK GUIDE TO CRAFT AND STRUCTURE (cont.)

Point of View

The ***point of view*** is the ***voice*** the novel is written in. The author's choice of a specific point of view for a novel relates to his or her purpose. The author may want readers to feel a deeper connection with one character and hear the story from just his or her perspective. Or the author may want the reader to have a more thorough understanding of all the characters and events in the story.

* **First-Person:** A character in the story is the narrator and describes what he or she sees, hears, feels, and thinks. The character uses words like "I" and "we." A first-person narrator can only tell the reader as much as his or her character knows.
* **Third-Person:** The narrator is not a character in the story. This type of narration does not use words like "I" and "we." The narrator is able to tell the reader what characters are doing, feeling, thinking, or saying. Third-person can be omniscient or limited. An ***omniscient*** narrator can describe any events and also all of the thoughts and actions of every character. A ***limited*** third-person point of view still uses "he" and "she" but describes situations in which the main character is involved.

INTERACTIVE LITERATURE NOTEBOOK SUGGESTIONS FOR UNIT 5

1 You'll Love It!	2 This Sentence Says It All	3 How It Made Me Feel	4 A Collection of Similes	5 Found Poem
Do you know somebody who would love the style of this book? Write a note to the person explaining why you think he or she will enjoy this book.	As you read, look for sentences that stand out and are meaningful to you. Create a page of your favorite quotations from the book.	How did this book make you feel as you read it? Create a page of words, pictures, and colors that describe the tone of the book.	A simile is a figure of speech that uses *like* or *as* to compare two unlike things that have something in common. *Home of the Brave* uses many similes to add emphasis or description to the poems. Create a page of some of the similes you find in the book. Write down the similes and their meanings. Include pictures.	Imagine that one of the characters in *Home of the Brave* finds one of the poems Kek has written. Write a paragraph from that character's point of view reacting to the poem.

AFRICAN PROVERBS

Katherine Applegate organized *Home of the Brave* into four parts and an epilogue. She uses an African proverb at the beginning of each section. A **proverb** is a short saying that contains advice that explains an accepted truth about life. Consider why the author does this and how each proverb can also apply to *A Long Walk to Water*.

Some proverbs use metaphors or symbolism. For example, the expression "The early bird catches the worm" is a famous proverb that uses figurative language to make a point. This saying is not really about birds and worms. What do you think this proverb means?

_____

_____

Now discuss how the author used African proverbs in *Home of the Brave*. Read these proverbs and think about the message and symbolism in each one. For each proverb, do the following to fill in the charts below and on the next page:

- Write the proverb as it appears in *Home of the Brave*. The first one is written for you.
- Explain what the proverb means.
- Explain how the proverb's message can apply to each of the major characters in these two novels: Kek, Salva, and Nya.

"Part One" Proverb (from page 1)	"When elephants fight, it is the grass that suffers."
Meaning	
How this applies to Kek	
How this applies to Salva	
How this applies to Nya	

"Part Two" Proverb (from page 51)	
Meaning	
How this applies to Kek	
How this applies to Salva	
How this applies to Nya	

AFRICAN PROVERBS *(cont.)*

"Part Three" Proverb (from page 129)	
Meaning	
How this applies to Kek	
How this applies to Salva	
How this applies to Nya	

"Part Four" Proverb (from page 225)	
Meaning	
How this applies to Kek	
How this applies to Salva	
How this applies to Nya	

"Part Five" Proverb (from page 243)	
Meaning	
How this applies to Kek	
How this applies to Salva	
How this applies to Nya	

Name: _____

STUDYING WRITER'S CRAFT

Think about the way the authors organized each novel. How do the stories unfold? Look through each book and discuss how chapter length changes the way you read the novels. The authors of *A Long Walk to Water* and *Home of the Brave* both use flashbacks to help tell their stories. Both authors also build suspense by using cliffhangers. Look closely at these techniques as you compare the novels.

Flashbacks

Find an example of a flashback in each novel and explain how its use helps tell the story.

Novel	A Long Walk to Water	Home of the Brave
Example		
Page number		
Explanation		

1. Which book uses more flashbacks? _____

2. Why do you think flashbacks are more important to the storytelling in this book?

_____

_____

Building Suspense through Chapter Cliffhangers

Find an example of building suspense in both novels and explain how its use affects the way the reader reacts to the story.

Novel	A Long Walk to Water	Home of the Brave
Example		
Page number		
Explanation		

3. Which novel do you think is more suspenseful? _____

4. Explain your previous answer. What did that author do to accomplish this?

_____

_____

_____

WHOSE POINT OF VIEW?

A Long Walk to Water and *Home of the Brave* are written in different points of view. The point of view changes the way the story is told. It also affects how much the reader knows about all the characters. Think about what would change if the novel were told from a different point of view.

1. If *A Long Walk to Water* had been written from only Salva's point of view instead of third-person, what parts of the story would need to be taken out?

   _____

   _____

2. What do those parts add to the story? _____

   _____

   _____

3. *Home of the Brave* is written in first-person, from Kek's perspective. What if it had been written in a third-person point of view like *A Long Walk to Water*? What other details do you think could have been added to the novel that Kek would not have known?

   _____

   _____

   _____

4. Do you think you would understand Kek's feelings as well if the story were written in third-person? Explain why.

   _____

   _____

5. Would changing the story to third-person make the story better or worse? Explain.

   _____

   _____

6. As you read, did you feel that you got to know Kek or Salva better? Explain.

   _____

   _____

Think about the way point of view fits the story. Authors choose the point of view that works best for the story they want to tell. However, readers may still prefer one type to the other. What is your preference?

I prefer books written in _____-person point of view because _____

_____

_____

Name: _____

WHAT'S LEFT UNSAID

Use inference to figure out information the author does not state in *A Long Walk to Water*.

1. Reread Salva's section of Chapter Four that begins on page 21 and ends at the top of page 22. Summarize what the text <u>says</u> happened in this section. Focus on what happened, not why.

   _____

   _____

   _____

2. The woman who touches the arm of one of the men never says anything. What can you (and the man) infer she is thinking?

   _____

   _____

3. Who do you think the man is? _____

4. The man says he is taking Salva because he is Dinka. Do you think that is the only reason? Explain.

   _____

   _____

Now use inference to figure out information the author does not state in *Home of the Brave*.

5. Reread "Goodbyes" (pages 25–28). Summarize what happens in this passage.

   _____

   _____

   _____

6. How does Kek act toward Dave, his aunt, and Ganwar in this scene?

   _____

   _____

7. How does Kek really feel about his situation?

   _____

   _____

8. What information/clues in this passage did you use to help you make this inference?

   _____

   _____

9. Why do you think Kek does not say how he really feels?

   _____

   _____

IDENTIFYING TONE

The author chooses words and sentence structure to create the *tone* of the book or scene. The tone may change several times in the novel, depending on what is happening in the scenes. You and your partner will read a passage in each novel and discuss the tone in that scene. Work together to identify how each author selects words and phrases to create a feeling about the author's or character's attitude.

Compare the tone in the following passages:

Novel	*A Long Walk to Water*	*Home of the Brave*
Passage	"Six years later: July 1991"	"Sleep Story"
Pages	73–75	198–200
What is the tone of this passage?		
Identify the words and phrases that help you determine the tone.		

1. How are these two scenes similar? _____

_____

_____

2. Why do you think the authors use this type of tone at this point in the story?

_____

_____

_____

Cite an example of a completely different tone of a passage in one of the novels.

Novel: _____

Passage: _____ Page numbers: _____

What is happening in this passage? _____

_____

What is the tone? _____

Identify words and phrases that help you determine the tone.

_____

_____

FORM FLIP

Home of the Brave tells Kek's story through a series of poems. Look at the poem "Mama" (pages 47–48). Select a few lines of this poem that you think are particularly powerful or vivid.

Quote them here: _____

_____

_____

_____

Page number: _____

1. What makes these lines a good example of poetic form?

_____

_____

_____

2. Think about the way poetry affects the reader and conveys Kek's feelings. Why do you think the author chose to write Kek's story in poetry rather than prose?

_____

_____

_____

A Long Walk to Water is told in prose. Review Chapter 8, particularly Salva's memories of his father bringing home mangos. Find a short passage (2–3 sentences) from *A Long Walk to Water* that you think shows good use of prose.

Quote them here: _____

_____

_____

_____

Page number: _____

3. What makes these sentences a good example of prose form?

_____

_____

_____

FORM FLIP (cont.)

What if *A Long Walk to Water* had been written as a verse novel? What if Kek's story in *Home of the Brave* had been told in traditional prose rather than free-verse poetry? Do you think the reader's experience would be very different? To get a better understanding of the way form affects story, first try to rewrite a short passage from each book in a different form.

Novel: _____ *Home of the Brave* _____

Poem: _____ "Mama" _____ **Pages:** ___47–48___

Rewrite this part of the novel as if Kek were describing his mother in a paragraph, not poetry. How would he describe her and his feelings about her?

_____

_____

_____

_____

_____

Novel: _____ *A Long Walk to Water* _____

Chapter: _____ Eight (the mango memory) _____ **Page:** ___48___

Write this scene as a poem. Try using key words and phrases from the passage to help you get started.

_____

_____

_____

_____

_____

_____

1. Would *A Long Walk to Water* work as well if it were written in poetry? Explain.

_____

_____

2. Would *Home of the Brave* work as well if it were written in prose? Explain.

_____

_____

UNIT 6 TEACHER INSTRUCTIONS

The worksheets contained in the previous units give students practice in applying knowledge of literary elements to the novels they read. To further develop their ability to analyze literature as well as their fluency in writing, students need opportunities to produce more in-depth work. Longer writing assignments and projects promote deeper comprehension of both the novels specifically and the way literary elements function in general.

In this unit, students will extend their learning by producing creative projects and analytical essays that are focused, organized, and well developed. The essay assignment sheets guide students through the writing process—from brainstorming, to planning, to drafting, to editing.

Unit 6 includes the following components. See page 5 of this book for an explanation of icons.

 "Welcome to America" (page 55) — Practice narrative writing and reflect on the messages in these novels through short story.

 "Country Scrapbook" (pages 56–57) — Use information from interviews, research, and both novels to create a comprehensive scrapbook of information on family history and the immigrant experience.

 "Comparing a Theme" (page 58) — Use a traditional essay format to compare the themes of the two novels. Plan the essay on the worksheet provided, including finding relevant quotations to support points. Drafts are written on a separate piece of paper.

 "Comparing Genre and Form" (pages 59–60) — Write an informative essay that compares the forms of the two novels. Complete a prewriting worksheet to generate ideas and find a focus for a comparison essay. Use the model format to help plan and draft an essay.

 "Self-Editing Checklist (Rough Draft)" (page 61) — Use this checklist to stay on task and organized after the completion of an essay's first draft.

(*TIP:* This resource may be used with both the "Comparing a Theme" and the "Comparing Genre and Form" essay assignments.)

 "Peer-Editing Checklist" (page 62) — Use this checklist to evaluate the essays of other students and to receive feedback about essays prior to completing a final draft.

(*TIP:* This resource may be used with both the "Comparing a Theme" and the "Comparing Genre and Form" essay assignments.)

 "Self-Editing Checklist (Final Draft)" (page 63) — This checklist should be used to fine-tune essays and to implement the suggestions given by peers.

(*TIP:* This resource may be used with both the "Comparing a Theme" and the "Comparing Genre and Form" essay assignments.)

Name: _____

WELCOME TO AMERICA

Imagine a young refugee from Sudan moves into your neighborhood. Like Salva and Kek, he is unfamiliar with American life and does not understand some of the expressions we use when we talk.

➤ First, imagine this character (age, appearance, etc.).

➤ Decide the location in which you meet him (school cafeteria, park, bus stop, etc.).

➤ Who is with you when you meet the new neighbor? Are you alone or are you with friends or family?

Now write a short story that describes this situation. What would you say and do? How do you think he would respond? Use dialogue and details to create characters and a sequence of events.

_____
_____
_____
_____
_____
_____
_____
_____
_____
_____
_____
_____
_____
_____
_____
_____
_____
_____
_____

COUNTRY SCRAPBOOK

A Long Walk to Water and *Home of the Brave* tell stories of refugees leaving Sudan to escape war. The United States is frequently referred to as a melting pot because it is made up of people who originally came from all over the world. With the exception of Native Americans, every American has ancestors from another country. Some of those relatives came to the U.S. to escape war or poor conditions in their homeland. Others came seeking opportunities. For this project, you will create a scrapbook about your own family's country of origin.

Find out about your family's origins. Ask your parents, grandparents, or great-grandparents to tell you about your family's history. Some students, like Kek, may have come to the U.S. very recently and are the first ones in their family to become Americans. Other students may have grandparents who came from other countries. Other families may have come to the United States so long ago that the family is not sure when their ancestors first arrived.

Many people in the United States have ancestors from more than one country. Perhaps your great-grandmother was from Italy and your great grandfather's family was originally from Spain. If your family has ancestors from more than one country, pick one country to research. Ask your family which ancestors they know the most about. If your family is Native American, write about the history of your family's tribe.

Complete the form below, using the information given to you by your family members. It's okay if your family does not know the answers to all the questions.

The country I will research is _____.

Statements	Notes
1. Our family first came to the United States in _____. (year)	If you don't know for sure, what do your parents or grandparents think is a good guess?
2. The family members who first came to the U.S. were _____ _____.	Did one person come first, or did several members of your family travel here together?
3. My family first moved to the U.S. for this reason: _____ _____.	What was the main reason for which your family member(s) moved to the U.S.?
4. When my ancestors first moved to the United States, they _____ _____ _____.	Where did they live? What jobs did they do?

Name: _____

COUNTRY SCRAPBOOK (cont.)

Do research on your country. Find out facts about the country and its history. Take notes, using the outline below as a guide. Also find pictures, images, stickers, and any small items to make your scrapbook creative and interesting to look at. If you have old pictures of your relatives, ask your parents to make a photocopy for you to include in your scrapbook. Plan out each page before you glue anything down.

Section 1: Information about the Country

Included in this section:

❏ a map of the country

❏ facts on the location, size, and population

❏ timeline of important historical events

❏ information about culture, such as the following: language, food, holidays, style of dress, music, traditions, famous people

Section 2: Personal Connections

In this section, write a paragraph for each question and decorate your page to match the ideas.

❏ If you know when your family left this country, write a one-paragraph explanation of what was happening in the country at this time that may have led to your family leaving. If you do not know exactly when your family left, pick one major conflict or crisis in this country's past and write a one-paragraph summary of what happened and why it may have caused people to leave the country.

❏ Do you still have relatives living there? If so, give facts about where they live and what they do. If not, would your family like to visit this country? Explain.

❏ Imagine you are going to move to this country next week. Write a paragraph describing what you think would be the hardest and easiest things to get used to.

Section 3: Novel Connections

❏ Imagine Kek and Salva immigrated to this country instead of the United States. Describe what other things they may have had to get used to or what would have been easier for them.

❏ Think about what your relatives might have experienced when they moved from this country to the U.S. How do you think their experience would have been similar to Kek and Salva's move to the U.S.? How would it have been different?

COMPARING A THEME

Write an essay that compares the way each book addresses a specific theme. To compare two novels in a subject-by-subject essay, first start with your claim about the theme in both books. Then, in the body paragraphs, discuss one book at a time. Plan your essay here and then write out your draft on a separate sheet of paper.

A Long Walk to Water and *Home of the Brave* share several important themes about war, family, perseverance, hope, and adapting to change. Which of these themes do you think is the most important theme in both novels?

I. **Introduction Paragraph: Your Claim**

- What do these novels show readers about the topic you selected?

   _____

II. **Examples from *A Long Walk to Water***

- How does *A Long Walk to Water* show this theme?

   _____

   _____

- Give at least one quotation as evidence.
- Explain why this quotation is important.

III. **Examples from *Home of the Brave***

- How does *Home of the Brave* show this theme?

   _____

   _____

- Give at least one quotation as evidence.
- Explain why this quotation is important.

IV. **Conclusion Paragraph**

- Why is this theme important for readers to understand?
- Are the books more similar or different in the way they present this theme?

TIP: When you write your essay, be sure to use phrases that show comparison and contrast. Here are some examples:

Similar to	Like	Compared to
However	Unlike	In Contrast

Name: _____

COMPARING GENRE AND FORM

Prewriting Worksheet

You will use the following pages to plan and write a a point-by-point comparison essay. In order to write this type of essay, you start with a claim about both novels. Each body paragraph of your essay focuses on one similarity or difference between the novels and uses examples from both novels.

Begin by brainstorming ideas. How are the books similar even though one is prose and one is poetry? List as many ideas as you can think of.

_____

_____

_____

How is reading a story told through poetry different from reading one told in prose?

Here are some ideas to help you get started:

- Did one form help you understand the character's feelings better?

- Did one form make the story feel more complete?

- Did poetry make the book easier or more difficult to read than prose?

_____

_____

_____

Thesis Statement Starter

Look through your notes above and decide what similarities and differences you want to write about. What do you want to tell readers about the differences in reading a book in prose versus a book in poetry? Use your thoughts to construct a thesis statement, from which your entire essay will follow. The following sample will help you to do this:

Although *A Long Walk to Water* is written in prose and *Home of the Brave* is written in verse, they both

_____

However, telling the story through poetry _____

_____

_____

COMPARING GENRE AND FORM (cont.)

Create an outline for your essay. Write down key words and ideas here.

I. Introduction

Introduce your essay. Provide the thesis, from which the entire essay will follow.

_____

_____

_____

II. First Point

Pick one similarity or difference. Name it here: _____

_____

    A. Provide an example from *A Long Walk to Water*.

    B. Provide an example from *Home of the Brave*.

    C. Explain how the two novels are similar or different.

III. A Second Point

Pick another similarity or difference. Name it here: _____

_____

    A. Provide an example from *A Long Walk to Water*.

    B. Provide an example from *Home of the Brave*.

    C. Explain how the two novels are similar or different.

IV. A Third Point

Pick another similarity or difference. Name it here: _____

_____

    A. Provide an example from *A Long Walk to Water*.

    B. Provide an example from *Home of the Brave*.

    C. Explain how the two novels are similar or different.

V. Conclusion

Wrap up your essay. Connect all the points together and sum up your thoughts.

Name: _____

SELF-EDITING CHECKLIST (ROUGH DRAFT)

Use this checklist to make sure your rough draft has everything that is required. Check off the box next to each item once you have included that element in your essay.

❏ My introduction states the topic of my essay and the point I will make about it.

❏ I have used quotations from *A Long Walk to Water*. How many? _____

❏ I have used quotations from *Home of the Brave*. How many? _____

❏ I have included page numbers of quotations from the novels.

❏ I have explained all quotations.

❏ I have used transition words that show comparison and contrast.

❏ My conclusion states the importance of my topic.

❏ My conclusion explains how the books are similar or different.

❏ I read over my essay to check for spelling, punctuation, and grammar mistakes.

One thing I like about my essay is _____

_____

_____

_____

One thing I am not sure about is _____

_____

_____

_____

One thing I need help with is _____

_____

_____

_____

PEER-EDITING CHECKLIST

Reader's Name: _____   Writer's Name: _____

Read your partner's essay and check a box for each statement.

	Yes	No
The introduction does a good job explaining the point the writer will make.	❏	❏
There are quotations from *A Long Walk to Water* in this essay.	❏	❏
How many? _____		
There are quotations from *Home of the Brave* in this essay.	❏	❏
How many? _____		
The essay uses the right comparison words and phrases to help show the relationship between ideas. (If there are any places that need more of these types of phrases, then mark them on the paper.)	❏	❏
The conclusion explains why the topic is important.	❏	❏
The conclusion makes sense and fits the rest of the essay.	❏	❏
There are no spelling errors or sentence mistakes.	❏	❏

Look closely at how well the writer explained each point. The paragraph that does this best is #_____.

Why? _____

_____

_____

A paragraph that is confusing or unclear is #_____. What questions did you have about this paragraph?

_____

_____

What did you like best about this essay? _____

_____

_____

What is one more thing the writer can do to make the paper better? _____

_____

_____

Name: _____

SELF-EDITING CHECKLIST (FINAL DRAFT)

After your peer editor or editors read your paper and give you comments, use those comments and suggestions to revise your essay.

> *TIP:* After you revise your paper, try reading it out loud one more time. Sometimes it is easier to find mistakes when you read your essay out loud to yourself.

Answer these questions after your final draft is complete.

(Circle one.) My first draft had   **no   some   many**   spelling and grammar mistakes.

I am still not sure about _____

_____

_____

_____

_____

After reading the comments on my paper, I added _____

_____

_____

_____

_____

The most important change I made on my draft was _____

_____

_____

_____

_____

INTRODUCTION TO SECTION II

The worksheets in the first section of this book encourage your students to make connections between the novels and think deeply about the way these novels approach similar topics and themes. The main goal of this book is to provide a wide range of activities that require students to compare the ideas, craft, and structure of these works.

Before your students can complete the activities that make up the focus of this book, they must first read and study each novel separately. To that end, the contents in this section are intended to provide you with single-novel activities that relate to concepts your students will encounter in the comparison activities. This section is not a comprehensive packet of single-novel worksheets, but rather it is a brief supplement that can be used in conjunction with the Interactive Notebook activities, your own single-novel activities, or other single-novel study guides.

In addition to the worksheets in this section, the Interactive Literature Notebook suggestions at the beginning of Units 1–5 will provide your students with creative ways to reinforce their understanding of literary elements in general and comprehension of these novels specifically. These Interactive Literature Notebook ideas provide you with a wide range of options for reinforcing your teaching of story elements and structure as you and your students read each novel.

The single-novel activities are divided into three units:

Unit 7 — pages 65–70

This unit includes individual activities that can be used with either novel. To get started, see the Teacher Instructions on page 65.

Unit 8 — pages 71–81

This unit includes activities specifically tailored to be used with *A Long Walk to Water*. To get started, see the Teacher Instructions on page 71.

Unit 9 — pages 82–92

This unit includes activities specifically tailored to be used with *Home of the Brave*. To get started, see the Teacher Instructions on page 82.

UNIT 7 TEACHER INSTRUCTIONS

The worksheets in this section provide general practice activities for use with either or both novels. All activities in this section are individual activities, although several can be adapted easily for collaborative or whole-class discussion.

Unit 7 includes the following components. See page 5 of this book for an explanation of icons.

"My Word Wall" (page 66) — Identify unknown words while reading. Practice using context clues as well as reference materials to understand word meaning.

(*TIP:* You may want to have each student suggest a word from his or her worksheet to create a Class Word Wall for further study and testing.)

"An Important Event" (page 67) — Build summarization skills and increase understanding of story elements. Examine how a specific scene relates to the overall structure of the story.

"What If?" (page 68) — This activity is a follow-up exercise based on the worksheet "An Important Event." Use it to further develop an understanding of how a scene or chapter affects the overall story.

"Writing a Persuasive Letter" (page 69) — Use a letter-writing format to construct an argument and support that opinion with evidence from the text.

(*TIP:* Have students share their letters with each other for proofreading and editing practice.)

"My Book Rating" (page 70) — Use a rating system to evaluate different components of the story before making a final evaluation of the book as a whole.

Name: _____

MY WORD WALL

Find your own vocabulary words. As you read the novel, look for words you don't know. Use this chart to write down the words and their meanings.

My Own Sentence	Dictionary Definition	My Guess	Sentence and Page Number	Word

Name: _____

AN IMPORTANT EVENT

The plot is the series of events that make up the story. The author carefully creates events that show how the conflict, or main problem, of the story builds and resolves. Each point in the plot is important to the overall structure of the story. Think about how the events in the book fit together to tell the whole story.

Select one important event in the novel to analyze.

What are the page numbers of this scene? _____

Which characters were involved? _____
_____

Summarize what happens in this scene. _____
_____
_____
_____
_____

What caused the event in this scene? Why did it happen? _____
_____
_____
_____

Find one quotation that is important to the scene. _____
_____
_____

Page number: _____

Why is this an important scene? How does it fit the whole story?

_____
_____
_____
_____
_____
_____

Name: _____

WHAT IF?

In the last activity, you picked one event that is part of the plot and explained why it was important to the overall story. Further explore this event and its impact on the overall novel.

How does that scene end? _____

_____

_____

_____

_____

Why do you think it ends that way? _____

_____

_____

_____

Think of another way this scene could have ended. Describe the new ending here.

_____

_____

_____

_____

If the scene ended that way, how would the rest of the story change?

_____

_____

_____

_____

Would this change make the story better or worse? Explain why.

_____

_____

_____

_____

_____

Name: _____

WRITING A PERSUASIVE LETTER

Imagine a school in another town is considering using this novel in their 6th- and 7th-grade classes. They want to hear from students who have read the book and find out what they think. Write a letter to the school board explaining why you would or would not recommend this novel for their school. What do you like or not like about the writing? How do you think other kids will relate to the book?

Follow this outline and write your letter on a separate piece of paper.

Paragraph 1 should include this information:

- State whether or not you recommend the book.
- Explain your experience with the book. (When did you read it? Why did you read it? What did you think as you read it?)

Paragraph 2 should include this information:

- Explain one thing you thought was good or bad about this book. You can talk about style, characters, plot, theme, point of view, or any other writing-related topic.
- Give one example from the book that demonstrates your point.

Paragraph 3 should include this information:

- Explain another thing you liked or did not like about this book. Select from the same writing-related topics listed in the Paragraph 2 instructions.
- Give one example from the book that demonstrates your point.

Paragraph 4 should include this information:

- Explain how you think the students will respond to this book. Focus on the way it will make them feel or think about the situation described in the novel.
- Give one example from the book and explain how you felt when you read it.

Paragraph 5 should include this information:

- Write a conclusion that restates your recommendation and explains why it is important.

Dear School Board,

Paragraph 1 goes here.

Paragraph 2 goes here.

Paragraph 3 goes here.

Paragraph 4 goes here.

Paragraph 5 goes here.

Sincerely,

sign name ➔ *Your signature*

print name ➔ **Your name**

Name: _____

MY BOOK RATING

What did you like or dislike about this book? Think about the story elements and rank each one between 0 and 5 stars. Use the following rating scale:

0 stars	1 star	2 stars	3 stars	4 stars	5 stars
☆☆☆☆☆	★☆☆☆☆	★★☆☆☆	★★★☆☆	★★★★☆	★★★★★
terrible	bad	okay	good	great	amazing!

Characters

Reason: _____

Setting ☆☆☆☆☆

Reason: _____

Point of View ☆☆☆☆☆

Reason: _____

Plot ☆☆☆☆☆

Reason: _____

The Ending ☆☆☆☆☆

Reason: _____

Theme ☆☆☆☆☆

Reason: _____

Overall, I give this book _____ stars because _____

_____

_____

UNIT 8 TEACHER INSTRUCTIONS

The worksheets in this section provide activities intended specifically to be used with the novel *A Long Walk to Water*.

Unit 8 includes the following components. See page 5 of this book for an explanation of icons.

 "Character Changes" (page 72) — Understand character development and identify specific examples of character growth throughout the novel. Perform close readings of several chapters to determine how Salva goes from a child who is dependant on others, to a boy determined to survive, to a leader of other boys, and finally to the man devoted to saving the lives of the South Sudanese people.

 "Summarizing Stories" (page 73) — Write brief summaries of Salva's and Nya's stories. (*TIP:* Strong summary-writing skills are essential for college success, and students need practice in this type of writing.)

 "Describing Settings" (pages 74–75) — Examine how the author creates setting through specific details and descriptive words. After identifying examples, explain how the harsh conditions described in both Salva's and Nya's stories relate to the plot and purpose of the novel.

 "A War Within a War" (pages 76–77) — Consider the secondary conflict between the Dinka and Nuer tribes. Examine how this centuries-old conflict relates to access to water, and how Salva's actions at the end of the novel could lessen the tension between these tribes.

 "Create a Novel Poster" (page 78) — Collaborate to create a poster that identifies key points in a chapter and shows understanding of that chapter's relevance to the overall structure of the novel. (*TIP:* Divide the class into groups of 3 to 4 students and assign each group one of the chapters listed on the worksheet.)

 "Conduct a Gallery Walk" (page 79) — Generate questions and discussion based on the posters created in the previous activity. (*TIP:* Hang the posters around the room and have each group walk around to each poster. Give them sticky notes on which to write questions for each poster. When all the groups have walked around the room and written questions, have each group read and answer the questions on their poster.)

 "Historical Events, Fictional Accounts" (pages 80–81) — Work together to identify how the author weaves fact and fiction into the novel. Find information on the real Salva Dut and discuss the difference between reading a fictional account and reading informational texts.

Name: _____

CHARACTER CHANGES

Think about the way Salva changes from the beginning of the novel to the end. Review the chapters listed here and answer the questions.

Chapters One through Ten

1. How would you describe Salva at the beginning of the novel?

_____

_____

2. How do the adults he walks with treat him before Uncle Jewiir arrives? Why?

_____

_____

3. Find a quotation that shows how Salva thinks or feels at the beginning of the novel.

_____

_____

_____

Chapters Eleven and Twelve

4. After Marial and Uncle Jewiir are killed, how does Salva change?

_____

_____

5. Find a quotation that shows how Salva thinks or feels in these chapters.

_____

_____

_____

Chapter Thirteen

6. By the end of this chapter, how has Salva changed? How do others see him?

_____

_____

7. Find a quotation that supports your answer.

_____

_____

Chapter Seventeen

8. After 19 years apart, Salva finds his father. What kind of man has Salva grown into?

_____

_____

9. What is most important to Salva by the end of the novel?

_____

_____

Name: _____

SUMMARIZING STORIES

A *summary* is a short explanation of the main points of a longer work. To write a summary of a novel, use your own words to describe what the story is about. Do not include your opinion or reaction to the writing. Summaries simply report information.

A Long Walk to Water contains two separate stories that come together in the final chapter. Practice your summary-writing skills by writing a one-paragraph summary of Salva's story and a separate one-paragraph summary of Nya's story. Focus on the big ideas, not the details.

Salva's Story	Nya's Story
_____	_____
_____	_____
_____	_____
_____	_____
_____	_____
_____	_____
_____	_____
_____	_____
_____	_____
_____	_____
_____	_____
_____	_____
_____	_____

Now give your personal response. How did you feel about Salva's story and Nya's story? What did this novel make you think about?

_____

_____

_____

_____

_____

Name: _____

DESCRIBING SETTING

Most of *A Long Walk to Water* takes place in Africa during two different time periods. Examine how the author chooses words to create a vivid setting.

Salva's Story

Each chapter describes the events that happen to Salva as he flees from his village in search of safety. His journey takes him through lion country, across the Nile river, through countless miles of desert, to three refugee camps, and then to his new home in New York. The author uses descriptive words and specific details to create the setting. Identify three words or phrases that help you imagine the environment in each of these chapters.

	Words and Phrases	Page number
Chapter Two: fleeing the village		
Chapter Eight: the Nile village		
Chapter Nine: the Akobo desert		
Chapter Fourteen: Ifo refugee camp		
Chapter Sixteen: New York		

1. What is one thing that the African settings have in common?

_____

_____

2. What is the biggest difference between the African settings and the New York setting?

_____

_____

DESCRIBING SETTING (cont.)

3. How do the details help you understand what Salva experiences?

_____

_____

4. Do you think the author did a good job of helping the reader picture these places?

_____

5. Which description stands out to you as most memorable? Why?

_____

_____

_____

Nya's Story

Each chapter in the novel begins with Nya's story. Reread Nya's sections in Chapters One and Three. How does the author establish the setting? Identify three words or phrases that create a sense of place and help you imagine what the environment is like.

	Words and Phrases	Page number
Chapter One		
Chapter Three		

6. How would you describe Nya's daily walks to fetch water?

_____

_____

_____

7. How do these details help you understand what Nya experiences?

_____

_____

_____

A WAR WITHIN A WAR

This novel gives readers a glimpse into the horrors of war. In particular, the story focuses on the Second Sudanese Civil War that began in 1983 and ended in 2005. This conflict was between the government and rebels who wanted to keep their own religion and culture. However, the book also describes another important conflict between two Sudanese tribes.

Chapter Three explains Salva's fears about running into the Nuer tribe. Look in the chapter for information about the conflict between the Dinka and the Nuer.

1. Why are these two tribes in conflict? Be specific and detailed.

   _____

   _____

   _____

   _____

2. Why is this conflict so important to the lives of these tribes?

   _____

   _____

   _____

3. Provide a quotation that tells how long these two tribes have been fighting each other.

   _____

   _____

4. Now scan Nya's section in Chapter Five. What tribe is she from? _____

5. Why doesn't Nya's family live near the lake all the time?

   _____

   _____

6. What happens during the dry season that makes it safer to live near the lake?

   _____

   _____

   Provide a quotation that gives you this answer. (from page number: _____)

   _____

   _____

   _____

A WAR WITHIN A WAR (cont.)

The Dinka and the Nuer tribes are both being attacked by the government soldiers. Both Dinka and Nuer boys were forced to flee Sudan during this war. Reread the passage in which the Nuer men encounter Salva's group (Chapter Ten).

7. Why do you think the Nuer men rob Salva's group?

_____

_____

8. These men also murder Salva's uncle before they leave. Why do you think they killed Uncle, but no one else from the group? Could there be more than one reason? Explain.

_____

_____

_____

9. In the last chapter of the novel, Nya finds out that the man building the well is a Dinka. Why does this surprise her?

_____

_____

10. Nya notices that the assistants are all Nuer. Why do you think the Nuer are willing to work for a Dinka boss?

_____

_____

11. The last sentence of the novel reveals that the boss is actually Salva, who has returned to Sudan to provide water to the villages. He started with Dinka villages but now is bringing water to the Nuer. Did it surprise you that Salva would want to help the Nuer? Explain your answer.

_____

_____

_____

12. Look back at your answers on the first page of this worksheet. Explain how the nature of the conflict between the Dinka and the Nuer is related to Salva's work in the last chapter.

_____

_____

_____

_____

CREATE A NOVEL POSTER

Your group will work together to create a poster that represents one chapter of *A Long Walk to Water*. Your teacher will assign your group one of the following chapters.

Chapter One	Chapter Nine	Chapter Fifteen
Chapter Four	Chapter Twelve	Chapter Seventeen
Chapter Six	Chapter Thirteen	

Our group has been assigned Chapter _____.

First, your group should discuss the events in your chapter and decide which details are the most important.

Your poster should contain all of the following elements. Write down who will be in charge of each.

	Elements	Assigned to
1	▪ the number of the chapter ▪ a short explanation of what happens in this chapter (two or three sentences)	
2	▪ a quotation from this chapter ▪ a short explanation of the significance of the quotation	
3	▪ a picture representing the most important event in this chapter ▪ a short description of the event	
4	▪ a picture that represents the setting of this event ▪ a one-sentence explanation of where the event takes place	
5	▪ a picture that represents the feeling or mood of this scene ▪ a sentence or collage of words that represent the emotions in this chapter	

TIPS:

* **Be creative!** You may draw pictures, use pictures from magazines, print images from the Internet (with permission from your teacher), or paste on objects that relate to the story.

* **Plan before you start.** Everyone should collect pictures and ideas before anyone begins writing on the poster board. Work together to design the look of the poster by placing all pictures before you paste them. Don't forget to leave room for the written parts.

UNIT 8: ACTIVITIES FOR A LONG WALK TO WATER

Name(s): _____

CONDUCT A GALLERY WALK

Each group in your class has created a poster, and now these posters are on display. As a group, walk around your classroom and take a look at the posters created by the other groups. This is your chance to ask questions about each group's choices. It will also be your chance to answer questions about the choices you made when creating your group's poster.

Consider the following ideas when writing questions about other groups' posters:

Is an idea on the poster not clear?

Do You disagree with a point the poster makes?

Do You want more information about something the group has included?

Do You want to ask how the group felt about any particular scene or character?

Do You want to bring up something You thought was important in that section that isn't included on the poster?

Name(s): _____

HISTORICAL EVENTS, FICTIONAL ACCOUNTS

A Long Walk to Water is the fictionalized version of Salva Dut's amazing true story. Author Linda Sue Park based her novel on actual events, but she used her imagination to create the scenes, descriptions, and dialogue. You can find out more information about the real Salva Dut and his organization by visiting the website *http://www.waterforsouthsudan.org*. Explore the website, especially Salva Dut's biography on the "Who We Are" page. Also watch some of the videos on the website to get a better understanding of life in South Sudan and the importance of the wells Salva's organization is bringing to these villages.

Discuss the following questions with a partner. Record the main points of your discussion.

1. What surprised you about the information given on the website? What was most interesting?

   _____

   _____

   _____

   _____

   _____

   _____

2. How did reading about and watching the real story of Salva differ from the experience of reading the novel?

   _____

   _____

   _____

   _____

   _____

3. Linda Sue Park made up the character of Nya to show what living in South Sudan was like 20 years after Salva's story began. What is happening in Sudan in Nya's chapters?

   _____

   _____

   _____

   _____

   _____

HISTORICAL EVENTS, FICTIONAL ACCOUNTS (cont.)

You and your partner will now select a chapter from *A Long Walk to Water* and reread the events that happen to Salva. Discuss which details seem fictionalized. What information from the chapter seems like facts the author got through research? What details and descriptions seem like some the author wrote from her own imagination? Give three examples of each type.

Chapter _____

	Facts	Author's imagination
1.		
2.		
3.		

1. Now that you have done some research on the real events, do you think the author of *A Long Walk to Water* did a good job re-creating these events in the novel? Explain and give an example.

_____

_____

_____

_____

2. The novel is about Salva's journey and how he becomes a leader. The author could have described what happened to Salva without telling the reader about the history of the war. Why is it important for the author to include specific details and facts about the Sudanese civil war, the government, and the Dinka people in this story?

_____

_____

_____

_____

UNIT 9 TEACHER INSTRUCTIONS

The worksheets in this section provide activities intended specifically to be used with the novel *Home of the Brave*.

Unit 9 includes the following components. See page 5 of this book for an explanation of icons.

 "Transforming Form" (page 83) — Think about genre and point of view by rewriting a scene in prose rather than poetry and in the point of view of a different character. (*TIP:* After students complete the activity, select a few sample paragraphs or have volunteers read their paragraphs. Discuss the differences between prose and poetry, and how form affects the way we read.)

 "Sum It Up!" (pages 84–85) — After summarizing each of the four sections of the novel, think about the main purpose of each section and identify the unifying idea of each. Consider the author's reasons for structuring the book this way and create a title for each section. (*TIP:* If *Home of the Brave* is a read-aloud, stop after each section and allow students to write their summaries immediately. Before moving on to the next section, have students pair up to read their summaries to each other and then share a few examples with the whole class. Discuss what important events should be in each summary. If students are reading the novel on their own, have them complete the summaries for homework after they finish each section.)

 "Characterizing Cousins" (pages 86–87) — Learn the difference between static and dynamic characters. Through close reading and citing of evidence from the text, identify how Kek and Ganwar change and the effect each character has on the other.

 "Getting to Know Secondary Characters" (page 88) — Work in pairs to analyze a secondary character and create an interview. (*TIP:* Assign one of the secondary characters listed on the worksheet to each pair of students. Since there are not very many characters in the novel, you will most likely need to assign the same character to more than one group. This could allow for additional discussion of the types of questions each group created and the similarities or differences in their responses.)

 "Land of the Free" (page 89) — Consider how a famous poem quoted in the novel relates to the immigrant experience. Analyze language, explain meaning, and use quotations from *Home of the Brave* to show how the sentiment in this poem is both demonstrated and not demonstrated in the novel. (*TIP:* Practice poetry analysis by leading a whole-class discussion of the meaning of each line in "The New Colossus" by Emma Lazarus, the poem inscribed on the base of the Statue of Liberty. Focus on language, sound, and symbols. Then have students reinforce their understanding by answering the remaining questions on their own.)

 "Readers Theater" (pages 90–91) — Work in small groups to create a script dramatizing one poem or a few stanzas of a poem. (*TIP:* Distribute the "Writing a Script" handout on page 91 in order to show students the different components of a script.)

 "*Home of the Brave* Posters" (page 92) — Collaborate to create a poster that identifies poetic elements in one of the poems. (*TIP:* Use this activity in conjunction with the "Conduct a Gallery Walk" worksheet on page 79.)

Name: _____

TRANSFORMING FORM

Home of the Brave is a verse novel. The author tells Kek's story through free-verse poetry rather than prose. The novel still has a plot and characters like a prose novel, but the form of the novel is poetry. To prepare for this activity, reread the poem "Not-Smart Boy" (pages 99–101) about Kek's mistake with the washing machine.

Imagine you are Hannah. In the space below, rewrite this scene as a prose paragraph from Hannah's point of view. Describe what happened and what you (as Hannah) are thinking. Use a first-person voice.

_____

_____

_____

_____

_____

_____

_____

_____

1. What are the differences between your prose version and the original poem?

_____

_____

2. Think about why the author chose poetry rather than prose for Kek to tell his story. How does poetry fit the character and the story better than prose?

_____

_____

_____

3. How does this form change the way you read the book?

_____

_____

_____

Name: _____

SUM IT UP!

A *summary* is a short explanation of the main points of a longer work. To write a summary of a novel, use your own words to describe what happened in the story. Just include the most important points. Do not include your opinion or reaction to the writing. Summaries report the most important information.

Home of the Brave is separated into four parts, plus an epilogue. This activity will help you practice your summary skills and give you an opportunity to stop and reflect on each part of the novel. After you finish each section, stop and write a brief summary of what happened in that section. Focus on explaining the important events, not small details. Do not include your opinion.

Your summaries for Part One and Part Four should be very short. The longest section of the book is Part Three, so that summary should be a little longer.

Part One (pages 1–50)

_____
_____
_____
_____
_____

Part Two (pages 52–127)

_____
_____
_____
_____
_____
_____
_____
_____
_____

Name: _____

SUM IT UP! (cont.)

Part Three (pages 129–224)

_____
_____
_____
_____
_____
_____
_____
_____
_____
_____

Part Four (pages 227–242)

_____
_____
_____
_____
_____

Epilogue (pages 243–249)
(**Note:** Since the epilogue is very short, try to summarize it in one sentence.)

_____
_____

Now that you have summarized each section, think about why the author divided her book into sections. What ties each section together? Review each summary and think of a title for each section. The title should relate to the main point of that section. For instance, a title for the epilogue might be "Reunion" or "Welcoming Mama."

Part One: _____

Part Two: _____

Part Three: _____

Part Four: _____

Epilogue: _____

CHARACTERIZING COUSINS

A character can be *static* or *dynamic*. A *static character* does not change, while a *dynamic character* changes in some way. A dynamic character might start out as immature and selfish and change by the end of the story to become mature and thoughtful. Or a character might start out as a bully and eventually feel sorry for his actions and change his behavior. *Home of the Brave* has both static and dynamic characters. For instance, Dave and Ms. Hernandez are both kind, helpful, and good-humored at the beginning and end of the book. They do not change, so they are static characters. However, Kek and Ganwar both change in response to the things that happen in the novel. Answer the questions about these characters and find evidence from the text to support your answers. Be sure to include page numbers for quotations.

1. What was Kek like as a little boy in Sudan, before the fighting started?

_____

_____

_____

Find a quotation to support your answer and write it here.

_____

_____

Page Number: _____

2. What is Kek like when he first arrives in America?

_____

_____

_____

Find a quotation to support your answer and write it here.

_____

_____

Page Number: _____

3. What is Ganwar like when Kek first moves in with him?

_____

_____

_____

Find a quotation to support your answer and write it here.

_____

_____

Page Number: _____

CHARACTERIZING COUSINS (cont.)

4. What is Ganwar like at the end of the novel?

_____

_____

_____

Find a quotation to support your answer and write it here.

_____

_____

Page Number: _____

5. Why do you think Ganwar changed?

_____

_____

_____

6. Why does Kek try to run away?

_____

_____

_____

7. How does Ganwar help Kek regain his hope at the end of the novel?

_____

_____

_____

8. What does Kek realize in the poem "Changes" (pages 222–224)?

_____

_____

_____

9. Who do you think changes the most in the novel, Ganwar or Kek? Explain your answer.

_____

_____

_____

_____

GETTING TO KNOW SECONDARY CHARACTERS

Kek is the main character in *Home of the Brave*, but the other characters are important, too. The secondary characters help readers understand the main character better and help move the plot along. You and a partner will analyze one secondary character and create a mock interview that demonstrates the character's personality.

Your teacher will assign one of these secondary characters to you and your partner.

Ganwar	Lou	Dave
Aunt Nyatal	Ms. Hernandez	Mr. Franklin
Hannah		

Write your assigned character's name here: _____

You and your partner will present a live interview of your assigned character. One of you will pretend to be the character, and the other will be the interviewer. Work together to plan your interview. Write five questions you would like to ask your assigned character. Use questions that require more than a one-word answer. There are four question starters below to help you. Create your own question for #5.

1. Tell us about _____

2. What did you think when _____

3. How would you _____

4. Explain why _____

5. _____

_____

Be prepared! Discuss how the character would answer these questions. Practice your presentation.

TIPS:

* **Interviewer:** Give the audience a brief introduction to the character and explain how the character knows Kek.

* **Interviewee:** Pretend you are the character throughout the interview. Answer the questions as you imagine the character would answer them. You may also try to talk and act as you imagine the character would.

LAND OF THE FREE

Reread "Last Day" (pages 184–188). On the last day of school, Kek's teachers bring a cake with the Statue of Liberty on it. Ms. Hernandez reads the words on the cake, which are part of a poem inscribed on the pedestal of the Statue of Liberty.

Read the quotation on the cake (page 188). Write down any words you do not know and look up their definitions.

Words	Definitions

In your own words, explain what the Statue of Liberty quote means.

_____

_____

_____

Ms. Hernandez tells her students,

> "These are important words, she says.
> They mean that
> this is your country
> now and forever"

1. Does Kek feel this way at this point in the novel? Explain your answer.

_____

_____

2. Now reread "Field Trip" (pages 146–149). On page 148, what does Kek say surprises him most about America?

_____

_____

_____

3. How does Kek's observation about America's "tribes" fit the Statue of Liberty quote?

_____

_____

_____

READERS THEATER

Home of the Brave is a novel in verse. The novel tells Kek's story through a series of poems that give readers brief descriptions of images, emotions, and reflections. The story does not use as much detail or dialogue as a prose novel, but we still understand what happens in the story.

Your group will read one of the poems from *Home of the Brave* and write a script that dramatizes the poem or a part of the poem. Imagine what the characters said and did. Make up dialogue and act out your scene for the class.

The following poems work well for this assignment:

Poem	Page Numbers	Characters in Scene
"Family"	pages 20–22	4 people
"Night"	pages 43–46	2 people
"New Desk"	pages 66–69	4 people
"Lunch"	pages 76–78	4 people
"Lou"	pages 117–119	3 people
"Ganwar, Meet Gol"	pages 138–141	2–4 people
"Ganwar"	pages 213–217	2 people
"Zoo"	pages 238–242	4–6 people

Our chosen poem is _____.

What happens in this scene? (You may also take information from the poem that follows yours if you need additional material for your scene.)

_____

_____

_____

_____

Who are the characters in this scene?   **Who will play each character?**

_____   _____

_____   _____

_____   _____

What props will you use for your scene?

_____

_____

On a separate piece of paper, write a script for your scene. Write dialogue based on your understanding of the characters and events. Use the script format explained on the "Writing a Script" handout.

READERS THEATER (cont.)

Writing a Script

A *script* is a type of writing that is different from essays, stories, or poems. It is the written version of a play or performance that is acted out.

A script contains these parts:

* **Cast of Characters**

    This is a list of the characters in the script. A script has a list of all characters at the beginning. In the script, a character's name is put in all capital letters every time that character speaks.

* **Setting**

    This is where the scene takes place. A script includes a setting so the people putting on the performance know how to decorate the stage and what props they might need.

* **Dialogue**

    Dialogue is what the characters say. Most of your script will be dialogue. You do not need to put quotation marks around dialogue in a script.

* **Stage Directions**

    Add sentences that describe what the characters should be doing in the scene or other things that are happening besides dialogue. This information helps the actors know what to do. These sentences are not read or spoken out loud. Instead, the audience sees the actors perform these actions. Put these sentences in parentheses.

Here is an example of script format:

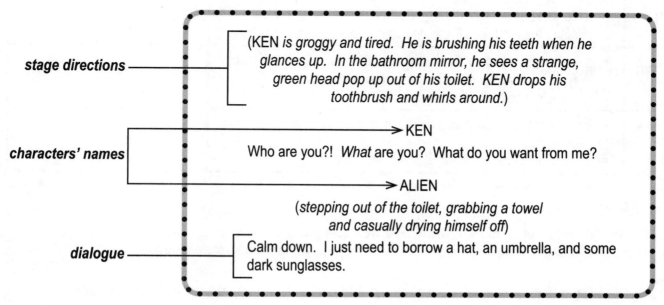

stage directions

(KEN *is groggy and tired. He is brushing his teeth when he glances up. In the bathroom mirror, he sees a strange, green head pop up out of his toilet. KEN drops his toothbrush and whirls around.*)

characters' names

KEN

Who are you?! *What* are you? What do you want from me?

ALIEN

(*stepping out of the toilet, grabbing a towel and casually drying himself off*)

dialogue

Calm down. I just need to borrow a hat, an umbrella, and some dark sunglasses.

HOME OF THE BRAVE *POSTERS*

Your group will work together to create a poster that analyzes one poem from *Home of the Brave*. Your teacher will assign your group one of the following poems:

> **"Sleep Story"** (pages 49–50)
>
> **"Once There Was"** (pages 63–65)
>
> **"Not Knowing"** (pages 81–84)
>
> **"Cowboy"** (pages 131–135)
>
> **"The Question"** (pages 150–151)
>
> **"Scars"** (pages 174–177)
>
> **"No More"** (pages 182–183)
>
> **"Changes"** (pages 221–224)

Our group has been assigned the poem titled _____.

First, your group should read the poem aloud so you can hear the sound of the language. One person may volunteer to read the entire poem, or several members may take turns reading stanzas.

Discuss the poetic elements and main idea of the poem. Take notes on your discussion. As a group, create a poster based on your poem. Your poster should contain all of the following elements. Write down who will be in charge of each.

	Elements	Assigned to
1	• the title of the poem • pictures or graphics to represent ideas, images, and tone of the poem	
2	• the main idea of the poem • a short explanation of the significance of the title (How does it relate to the main idea? Can the title mean more than one thing?)	
3	• a few examples of poetic devices in the poem and identification of type, such as figurative language (similes, metaphors, hyperbole, personification, symbols)	
4	• sound devices (repetition, alliteration, consonance, onomatopoeia, assonance) • word choice (connotations, sensory imagery, tone)	

TIPS:

* **Be creative!** You may draw pictures, use pictures from magazines, print images from the Internet (with permission from your teacher), or paste on objects that relate to the story.

* **Plan before you start.** Everyone should collect pictures and ideas before anyone begins writing on the poster board. Work together to design the look of the poster by placing all pictures before you paste them. Don't forget to leave room for the written parts.

COMMON CORE CORRELATIONS

The lessons and activities included in *Using Paired Novels to Build Close Reading Skills, Grades 6–7* meet the following Common Core State Standards. (©Copyright 2010. National Governors Association Center for Best Practices and Council of Chief State School Officers. All rights reserved.) For more information about the Common Core State Standards, go to *http://www.corestandards.org/* or visit *http://www.teachercreated.com/standards/* for more correlations to Common Core State Standards. (**Note:** When the standards are the same or nearly the same for both grade levels, their descriptions are listed only once.)

Reading: Literature	
Key Ideas and Details	**Pages**
ELA.RL.6.1 Cite textual evidence to support analysis of what the text says explicitly as well as inferences drawn from the text.	10, 12–14, 20, 22–24, 29–30, 32, 37–40, 42, 46–48, 50–52, 58–60, 67, 72, 74–76, 78, 86–87, 92
ELA.RL.7.1 Cite several pieces of textual evidence to support analysis of what the text says explicitly as well as inferences drawn from the text.	10, 12–14, 20, 22–24, 29–30, 32, 37–40, 42, 46–48, 50–52, 58–60, 67, 72, 74–76, 78, 86–87, 92
ELA.RL.6.2 Determine a theme or central idea of a text and how it is conveyed through particular details; provide a summary of the text distinct from personal opinions or judgments.	12, 20, 22–23, 25–26, 29–34, 37–42, 46–53, 58, 67, 72–77, 84–87, 89
ELA.RL.7.2 Determine a theme or central idea of a text and analyze its development over the course of the text; provide an objective summary of the text.	12, 15–16, 20, 22–23, 25–26, 29–34, 37–42, 46–53, 58, 67, 72–77, 84–87, 89
ELA.RL.6.3 Describe how a particular story's or drama's plot unfolds in a series of episodes as well as how the characters respond or change as the plot moves toward a resolution.	10, 12–16, 20–26, 29–32, 34, 38–42, 46–53, 58–60, 67–68, 72–77, 84–87, 89
ELA.RL.7.3 Analyze how particular elements of a story or drama interact (e.g., how setting shapes the characters or plot).	13–16, 20–26, 29–34, 37–42, 46–53, 58–60, 67–68, 72–77, 83, 86–87, 89
Craft and Structure	**Pages**
ELA.RL.6.4 / ELA.RL.7.4 Determine the meaning of words and phrases as they are used in a text, including figurative and connotative meanings.	*all activity pages*
ELA.RL.6.5 Analyze how a particular sentence, chapter, scene, or stanza fits into the overall structure of a text and contributes to the development of the theme, setting, or plot.	13–16, 20–26, 29–32, 34, 37–40, 42, 46–53, 58–60, 67–68, 72, 74–79, 89, 92
ELA.RL.7.5 Analyze how a drama's or poem's form or structure (e.g., soliloquy, sonnet) contributes to its meaning.	25, 46–49, 52–53, 59–60, 83, 92

COMMON CORE CORRELATIONS (cont.)

Reading: Literature (cont.)	
Craft and Structure (cont.)	**Pages**
ELA.RL.6.6 Explain how an author develops the point of view of the narrator or speaker in a text.	13–16, 20–24, 26, 30–34, 38–42, 46–50, 72, 74–77, 86–87, 89
ELA.RL.7.6 Analyze how an author develops and contrasts the points of view of different characters or narrators in a text.	13–16, 20, 22–23, 26, 30–31, 34, 38–42, 46–50, 74–77, 86–87
Integration of Knowledge and Ideas	**Pages**
ELA.RL.6.9 Compare and contrast texts in different forms or genres (e.g., stories and poems; historical novels and fantasy stories) in terms of their approaches to similar themes and topics.	20–23, 30, 37–41, 46–49, 51–53, 58–60, 83
ELA.RL.7.9 Compare and contrast a fictional portrayal of a time, place, or character and a historical account of the same period as a means of understanding how authors of fiction use or alter history.	30, 76–77, 80–81
Range of Reading and Level of Text Complexity	**Pages**
ELA.RL.7.10 By the end of the year, read and comprehend literature, including stories, dramas, and poems, in the grades 6–8 text complexity band independently and proficiently, with scaffolding as needed at the high end of the range.	*all activity pages*

Writing	
Text Types and Purposes	**Pages**
ELA.W.6.1. / ELA.W.7.1. Write arguments to support claims with clear reasons and relevant evidence.	*all activity pages*
ELA.W.6.2. / ELA.W.7.2. Write informative/explanatory texts to examine a topic and convey ideas, concepts, and information through the selection, organization, and analysis of relevant content.	*all activity pages*
ELA.W.6.3. / ELA.W.7.3. Write narratives to develop real or imagined experiences or events using effective technique, relevant descriptive details, and well-structured event sequences.	53, 55–57, 83, 90
Production and Distribution of Writing	**Pages**
ELA.W.6.4. / ELA.W.7.4. Produce clear and coherent writing in which the development and organization are appropriate to task, purpose, and audience.	*all activity pages*
ELA.W.6.5. / ELA.W.7.5. With some guidance and support from peers and adults, develop and strengthen writing as needed by planning, revising, editing, rewriting, or trying a new approach, focusing on how well purpose and audience have been addressed.	56–57, 59–63, 69

COMMON CORE CORRELATIONS (cont.)

Writing (cont.)	
Research to Build and Present Knowledge	**Pages**
ELA.W.6.7. / ELA.W.7.7. Conduct short research projects to answer a question, drawing on several sources and refocusing the inquiry when appropriate.	56–57, 80–81
ELA.W.6.8. / ELA.W.7.8. Gather relevant information from multiple print and digital sources.	*all activity pages*
ELA.W.6.9. / ELA.W.7.9. Draw evidence from literary or informational texts to support analysis, reflection, and research.	*all activity pages*
ELA.W.6.9A. Apply *grade 6 Reading standards* to literature (e.g., "Compare and contrast texts in different forms or genres [e.g., stories and poems; historical novels and fantasy stories] in terms of their approaches to similar themes and topics").	*all activity pages*
ELA.W.7.9A. Apply *grade 7 Reading standards* to literature (e.g., "Compare and contrast a fictional portrayal of a time, place, or character and a historical account of the same period as a means of understanding how authors of fiction use or alter history").	*all activity pages*

Speaking and Listening	
Comprehension and Collaboration	**Pages**
ELA.SL.6.1. / ELA.SL.7.1. Engage effectively in a range of collaborative discussions (one-on-one, in groups, and teacher-led) with diverse partners on grade 6 [and grade 7] topics and texts, building on others' ideas and expressing their own clearly.	11, 21–22, 24, 26, 30, 33, 37, 41, 46–47, 51, 78–81, 88, 90, 92
ELA.SL.6.2. / ELA.SL.7.2. Analyze the main ideas and supporting details presented in diverse media and formats (e.g., visually, quantitatively, orally) and explain how the ideas clarify a topic, text, or issue under study.	24, 33, 41, 78–81
ELA.SL.6.3. / ELA.SL.7.3. Delineate a speaker's argument and specific claims, distinguishing claims that are supported by reasons and evidence from claims that are not.	24, 33, 41
Presentation of Knowledge and Idea	**Pages**
ELA.SL.6.4. / ELA.SL.7.4. Present claims and findings, sequencing ideas logically and using pertinent descriptions, facts, and details to accentuate main ideas or themes; use appropriate eye contact, adequate volume, and clear pronunciation.	78–79, 88, 92
ELA.SL.6.5. / ELA.SL.7.5. Integrate multimedia and visual displays into presentations to clarify information, strengthen claims and evidence, and add interest.	78–79, 90, 92
ELA.SL.6.6. / ELA.SL.7.6. Adapt speech to a variety of contexts and tasks, demonstrating command of formal English when indicated or appropriate.	78–79, 88, 90, 92

COMMON CORE CORRELATIONS (cont.)

Language	
Conventions of Standard English	**Pages**
ELA.L.6.1. / ELA.L.7.1. Demonstrate command of the conventions of standard English grammar and usage when writing or speaking.	*all activity pages*
ELA.L.6.2. / ELA.L.7.2. Demonstrate command of the conventions of standard English capitalization, punctuation, and spelling when writing.	*all activity pages*
Knowledge of Language	**Pages**
ELA.L.7.3. / ELA.L.8.3. Use knowledge of language and its conventions when writing, speaking, reading, or listening.	*all activity pages*
ELA.L.6.4. / ELA.L.7.4. Determine or clarify the meaning of unknown and multiple-meaning words and phrases based on *grade 6 [and grade 7] reading and content*, choosing flexibly from a range of strategies.	*all activity pages*
Vocabulary Acquisition and Use	**Pages**
ELA.L.6.5. / ELA.L.7.5. Demonstrate understanding of figurative language, word relationships, and nuances in word meanings.	*all activity pages*
ELA.L.6.6. / ELA.L.7.6. Acquire and use accurately grade-appropriate general academic and domain-specific words and phrases; gather vocabulary knowledge when considering a word or phrase important to comprehension or expression.	*all activity pages*